A STUPID THING TO DO!

A meander up and down England and Scotland

by an old bloke on an even older bike

Noel Whittall

Propagator Press

This book is published by Propagator Press

Propagator Press
38 Parkside Road
Leeds
LS6 4NB

ISBN 978-1-908037-14-5

Designed by Propagator Press
Printed in Great Britain

For

Colin Missen

Contents

JOHN O' GROATS
INVERNESS
DALWHINNIE
PATHHEAD
LANARK
KIRKBY LONSDALE
RIPON
START AND FINISH
LEEDS
MATLOCK BATH
COVENTRY
BRISTOL
POACHER'S POCKET
OKEHAMPTON
LOSTWITHIEL
LAND'S END
100 MILES

Introduction

I reached my teens in the 1950s, so I did what we all did in those days: sought my freedom on a second-hand motorbike, a 1951 Francis Barnett Falcon. It was only a little two-stroke which was capable of about 55mph on a good day, but that was enough to keep me in love with motorcycles for more than fifty years. It has been a bit of an on-off affair at times, particularly from the 1970s when I allowed myself to be seduced by primitive flight – hang gliders, microlights, paragliders and paramotors, but all the time there was a motorcycle somewhere in the garage.

Since about the year 2000, flying began to take more of a back-seat and my involvement with early motorcycles has grown. During the decade I gradually wound down my occupation as a writer and editor and finally realised that I had retired and set out to make the most of it. All went fine for a year or so, with only a short pause for a skirmish with bladder cancer. With that safely out of the way thanks to the National Health Service, I resumed my new career of mild geriatric hedonism by learning to ski in winter and riding vintage bikes in as many events as possible during the summer. I also kept in touch with the sport of paragliding when the weather was particularly benign.

I have two Triumphs from the age when it was still easy to see that they were not much more than bicycles with simple motors added. One was made in 1913, the other 1918. They both drive the back wheel through a vee-belt, rather than a chain. I have a particular affection for the ex-military

1918 model. This was from the days before Triumphs had learned the marketing power of glamorous names such as 'Thunderbird' or 'Bonneville', so it is known simply as a 'Model H'. I rode mine frequently in many rallies for vintage bikes in England, Belgium and Germany. It is one of around thirty thousand that were delivered for despatch-rider work in the 1914-18 war.

Things came to a grinding halt one lovely autumn day in 2009, when I experienced a heart attack. There is little that is noble in the process, although I do claim to have pulled it off with at least a flourish of style, as I was piloting my paraglider more than a thousand feet up in the air above the ridge of Addingham Moorside at the time.

The flying was easy, the views were spectacular and I was taking air-to-air photos of my friend Pete as he flew nearby. Then, really quite gradually, I began to feel unwell and knew I would rather be on the ground. My arms felt heavy. I guided my wing toward Ilkley to lose height and then back to land in the heather above Addingham. I was very tired, but with a bit of help got the paraglider folded up, carried it about a mile across the moor to my car, drove home, took a couple of paracetamol and went to bed. I visited my doctor next morning and, to cut a long story short, came out of hospital more than two weeks later. Apparently I had a heart attack while in the air and by all accounts had been pretty lucky to have got away with it, although it took a hell of a lot of National Health Service skill and resources to get me back into running order again. They even had to use the jump leads on me at one stage.

Recovery took a long time, but I have been very lucky. When the hospital released me back into the wild I hadn't the strength to get out of a chair. I didn't think I had the slightest chance of riding motorcycles again. Some weeks of supervised exercise at a cardiac gym got me on my feet and I managed to complete the Pioneer Run from Epsom to Brighton on the 1913 Triumph in March '09, although I was pretty well finished at the end of it. Between then and the Vintage Motorcycle Club's flagship Banbury Run in June, based at the Heritage Motor Centre, I became ill again, but recovered sufficiently to participate and even finish with a cup for the best performance on an early Triumph. Nobody more surprised at that than me! I'd only gone into the prize-giving ceremony because there were loads of comfy chairs and I needed a good sit-down. With one or two setbacks I continued to get stronger and really enjoy life.

Now I wanted to see just what I could do and this End-to-End ride was my strange way of drawing a line under my year of dodgy health. And why a book? Well, I enjoy writing almost as much as cruising around on antiques and there is just a chance that all this might just encourage somebody else get up and do one of those slightly silly things that has been on their 'one day I'd like to …' shelf for ages.

Early motor cycle experiences

The route to my End-to-End ride was via more than 50 years of motorcycling. Much of this was done on vintage bikes because that was a cheap way to get into riding for sport many years ago.

1955 Still a teenager: my first trial, on a 197cc DMW in Sussex

1963 on my 1926 Model P Triumph at a Yorkshire VMCC trial. I paid £15 for it

1967 Getting off the line at the Esholt Sprint on Fred Willingham's much-modified Lambretta

Back to1966 at a hill climb at High Bradfield on a 1926 Norton.
I won theVintage class, but at the expense of a high-speed excursion into the farmyard midden through failure to stop!

1968 Trialling again, on a Sunbeam 350cc

1969 Vintage racing at Cadwell on a 1933 GP New Imperial

1969 Modern stuff: Esholt on a 160cc Honda

1970 In Italy at the top of the Colle Della Sommellier above Bardonecchia on a 1954 Triumph Tiger 100 which I assembled from a collection of parts

1973 on my R75/5 BMW in the Land's End Trial. I used this bike for almost every form of motorcycle sport for more than 30 years. It served me well and now appears in Vintage events in the hands of my good friend Bob McConnell

Chapter 1

The Golden Era Run

Sunday 27 September

At the Yorkshire Air Museum at Elvington about sixty ancient motorcycles lined up in the morning mist. They had gathered from far and wide and were waiting to be directed on a tour of the flatter parts of Yorkshire, over quiet roads suited to bikes which have become more than a handful to manage in the clamour of modern traffic. By ten o'clock the sun began to appear and the early starters were sent off. The sounds were those of a couple of generations ago as primitive engines were coaxed into life and a vague blue haze from hot oil replaced the earlier mist. This was the start of the Golden Era Run, an event which Ian Jennings and I had dreamed up in the cab of my rattley Nissan van while driving back from another old bike rally down in Essex a year earlier. Although there are many rallies for classic motorcycles we felt that the *really* old bikes, which frequently lack multiple gears, clutches, effective brakes and many of the accepted amenities of modern motorcycling, were being sadly neglected. We reckoned that there was space for a new event in the North which would cater fully for pre -1931 bikes only. Now here we were, making it happen, with the aid of a great crowd of fellow members of our section of the Vintage Motorcycle Club.

I cannot remember being so nervous since I first read a poem in public. Anyway, it all went very well, with fine weather and a cordial general mood. My son, Matthew, had visited from his home in Germany to ride my 1918 Model H Triumph, while Tim Britton, editor of *Old Bike Mart* newspaper, rode my 1913 Type C, also a Triumph. Both had trouble-free runs and afterwards we all gathered in the Museum's replica NAAFI for roast beef and Yorkshire pudding lunches. I felt a lot of responsibility as one of the main movers in getting the event started and had a great sense of relief once it was over.

Monday 28 September

I unloaded the pair of elderly Triumphs from my van to put them away for winter. I had a natural feeling of anticlimax after yesterday's success and it was with some regret that I wheeled the Model H, my favourite, into the garage, probably for the last time in the season. There are few vintage events organised once October has started. Never mind, I could concentrate on getting it into perfect condition over the winter. I would have the split in the petrol tank properly welded up – it was patched with a mass of quick-setting epoxy that I had slapped on a couple of years earlier. I would fit a new drive-belt rim to the rear wheel to replace the bent item which had been rather crudely straightened. And I would de-coke the engine and have a good look inside it. That was something I had intended to do for some time; it ran very well, but hadn't been inspected since I got it. Yes, it would be good to do all that, because then I would know that it was in as near-perfect condition as I could get it for next season. Deep at the back of my mind there was also lodged the idea that I would sometime fulfil one of my daydreams: riding an early vintage bike from Land's End to John o' Groats, or vice versa, and that would need a perfectly prepared bike and loads of spares, wouldn't it? Of course, it would have to be done in late spring or summer, to get the advantage of the long days and fine weather. It would be crazy to think of going at any other time. I looked at the H again. Next year seemed a long way away.

I had been thinking of making the 'End-to-End' trip for ages: something to do 'sometime'. I had even bought a couple of maps so that I could spread them out together on the floor and see mainland Britain in one piece and fantasise about efficient routes. Winter would give plenty of time to plan everything, organise backup, book over-night stops, prepare the bike fully, perhaps find a fellow rider or two and talk someone into driving a spares-and-workshop backup van. Or, just perhaps …

I slept on it.

Start of the adventure

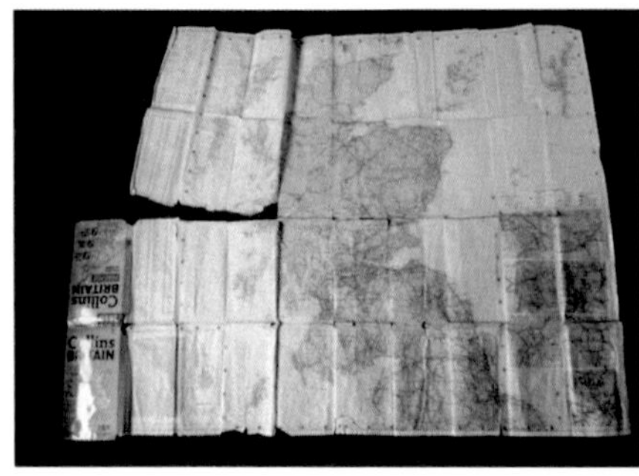

Maps tend to suffer a bit on a long wet motorcycle journey!

Chapter 2

Why not today?

Tuesday 29 September

'I suppose I could set off tomorrow', I told myself in the morning. I phoned Ian Jennings to take up his long-standing offer to lend me a spare pair of engine valves and springs, plus an extra spark-plug, and drove across the valley to see him and collect the parts. Ian had become an involuntary fellow conspirator because weeks before, when the idea had the barest breath of substance in my mind, I had asked him some very general questions about End-to-End rides. I also unguardedly remarked that a Land's End to John o' Groats run would be a fair road test of some new one-inch vee-link drive belting he had recently obtained and a sample of which I had fitted to the H. He took it all much more seriously than I did at the time and very kindly borrowed a wealth of reading material from VMCC Triumph expert Colin Missen. Colin had covered the course three times in the 1970s and 80s – twice on a 1911 single-geared belt-drive 500cc Triumph. He had followed routes established by record and rally riders from the heroic days before the Great War. I had read only part of his collection, intending to study it in depth during the winter as part of my extensive preparation.

On the way back from Ian's I began to realise that I might be going to attempt the journey much sooner than I originally had in mind. Did I really need to wait? I was ready for a small adventure and my health, which had been a bit dodgy, felt fine. The H was running well and over the years, I had already made several runs of 200 or more miles on it in a single day. After all, I reasoned, riding up to John o' Groats, down to Lands End and back up to Leeds was only a matter of stringing about ten such days together. And think of the advantages of simply setting off: no need for a backup vehicle; no need to trouble anyone else and it wouldn't be too ecologically unsound – a very small carbon-tyre print!

By the time I got home at lunchtime I *knew* I was going, but when, exactly? Autumn was well under way and I would need to get off soon. If tomorrow, why not today? I rang Trevor Birkbeck, a friend of many years, who lives out in the country a few miles north of Ripon. 'Can I blag your spare room tonight, Trev?' He agreed at once and I moved into top gear. Staying at Trev's would put me about 30 miles nearer to John o' Groats – a flying start! I went to a nearby outdoor equipment supermarket and bought a pair of bicycle panniers, a pulsing bicycle rear-light and a small groundsheet. About thirty quid the lot. Back home, I clipped and tied the lamp onto the reflective Sam Browne belt I planned to wear. A spare inner-tube, drive-belt and a litre tin of SAE 50 went into one pannier. The other took T-shirt, socks, underpants and an extra sweater. Also, a copy of Dan Brown's latest novel – not a brilliant choice as it turned out. The panniers were slung over an ancient doctors-type bag which contains tools and odds-and-ends and is a permanent resident on the carrier of the H. It all fitted quite well. A one-piece waterproof over-suit and the tarp were lashed on top with a cargo net, the tyres kicked in lieu of a pressure check, and she looked ready to go. Total preparation time two hours.

The over-suit was essential because the rest of my riding gear had undergone the test of many years and I knew full-well that it leaked. In fact the only part which doesn't leak is a side pocket on the Belstaff jacket, which retains water remarkably well. I wore padded leather motorcycle jeans and a pair of East-European jackboots which were excellent value when I bought them shortly after the fall of the Berlin Wall. At the last minute I debated whether to wear an elderly open-face helmet which reflects H's character quite well, or a more modern full-face one. Fortunately, I made probably the best decision of the whole escapade and went for the full-face. When I later rode past Glenshee where the first skiing of the season was under way and the snow-line almost within reaching distance, I blessed my choice.

A map, *Collins Britain Road Map 2010, 8.7 miles to the inch*, was tucked into the front of my jacket and off I went, meandering up the back roads to Ripon to arrive at Trev's in time for dinner. This was a bit delayed because his vast Aga stove was sulking. Trevor and his sister Judith produced a gourmet feed on a combination of Primus and microwave and we christened the stove the *Aga Khan't*. We had a great evening and my journey still had a feeling of unreality to it. I sat up in bed with the map and jotted down a possible route for the morning; Edinburgh should be within reach, given a bit of luck. H was tucked up in the garage with Trevor's 500T Norton for company.

I slept well.

Day's mileage: 31

I set out from home with oil and fuel tanks topped-up, but not absolutely brimming, because both tend to slop liquid out of the caps when going over bumps.

Approx 4.6 litres of petrol in the tank to start with.

Chapter 3

Up to Edinburgh (almost)

Wednesday September 30

One should have to pay money to ride up through the Yorkshire Dales early on an autumn morning. I was still on relatively familiar local roads which I had covered only a couple of weeks previously, but in a different role. Then Trevor had been on the H for his first belt-driver experience and I had been following in my aged Nissan van. We had enjoyed lunch at a rural pub, now gentrified and rather expensive, where H parked next to a drop-head Aston Martin and still drew all the attention in spite of her 90-plus years. Today, I was alone on H, with mist clearing over the River Ure before I climbed up to Middleham, where I drew up on meeting a string of race horses making for their stables after a spell on the gallops, but not, I fear, before we had rather surprised each other.

Then on through Richmond for my first fuel stop. H seems perfectly happy on cooking-grade unleaded and I was eager to see how much she would need. Richmond is about 60 miles from home by the route I had taken and she took slightly less than half a tankful. Not bad at all.

We were soon into Co Durham, making for West Auckland and the A68, that wonderful road that carves its way north, across the Wear and Tyne valleys and on up through the Scottish Borders. A Roman road, direct and uncompromising, each long climb followed by a steep descent calling for discipline if H were not to be allowed to over-rev. After a mellow start to the day, a strong northerly wind had set in and I struggled to remember that it was still September. As we motored towards Corbridge, the opening lines of W H Auden's *Roman Wall Blues* kept returning to me: ‘Over the heather the wet wind blows / I've got lice in my tunic and a cold in my nose / The rain comes pattering out of the sky / I'm a Wall soldier. I don't know why.’ I kept trying to recall the rest of the poem and found only fragments, but enough to let my mind range over just what life must have been like up here as a squaddie a couple of thousand years ago. The wind wasn't yet wet, but it was certainly blowing. It came straight down from Scotland with precious little to stop it.

Just past Otterburn, the A68 is joined by the road from Newcastle to climb up over the Cheviot Hills to the Scottish border at Carter Bar. It's a hard climb. Auden's wet wind is still blowing but it hasn't yet turned into proper rain. 'Services' are promised and I am in keen anticipation of a cup of tea, but there is only a bloody great rock welcoming us to Scotland and a distant view of a catering trailer over a wall on the other side of the dual carriageway. There was a kilted bagpiper over the other side too. On my side, just a plate with a few coins in it and a small note advising that the piper is not paid by the Scottish Tourist Board. There is probably a very sound reason for that.

Carter Bar wasn't all bad news: I enjoyed a brilliant few minutes with a family of Australian holidaymakers who seemed to be relishing the wet wind. They were fascinated by

H and my journey. In turn, I couldn't help remembering sailing in the warm breeze of Sydney harbour or watching mobs of parakeets squawking through the bush. At that particular moment I wasn't sure who had the best deal.

I had come this way on an ancient bike once before. The occasion was a York to Edinburgh rally sometime in the late 1970s. I was passenger in Keith Bastow's 1919 Royal Enfield sidecar outfit. The weather had started out perfect and there was very little for me to do in the chair as we chugged up north. I remember watching how the cloudless sky steadily became criss-crossed with aircraft vapour trails which widened out and gradually transformed into a sheet of cirrus from horizon to horizon, cutting out the sun. At the time it struck me that this was a clear example of human activity directly affecting climate, an image which has remained with me as the debate about global warming has developed. Of course, the closure in 1981 of the steelworks at Consettt, which used to dominate the view along miles of the A68, and the end of heavy industry along the Tees, Wear and Tyne valleys – all crossed by it – mean that today a lot less smoke is going into the atmosphere. I don't know which is better or worse, but Britain is certainly very different from what it must have been like when H left the factory. Ironically, before I reached my overnight stop, the road would lead us between the halves of the biggest on-shore wind farm in Europe, at the edge of the Lammamuir hills overlooking the Firth of Forth.

The demands of the inclines of the Cheviots and Southern Uplands made the belt slip and I had to take a link out at Jedburgh, where I also refuelled. Extracting or replacing links is never fun, but is the price to pay for the magical smoothness of belt drive. Shortly after this we were going along in fine style when a mid-twenties Bentley overtook us with a wave, followed by that glorious hollow booming exhaust note of a vintage sports car being allowed its head.

Whenever the road was fairly flat, H's exhaust beat always settled to the same rhythm and I found myself repeatedly fitting the words of an old folk song, *Hunting the Wren*, to it. It was my own fault: a day or two before setting out, I had unearthed a long-forgotten cassette of Steeleye Span. While not an I-pod man I have at least moved into the CD generation and hadn't played a cassette for years. Out of sheer curiosity I decided to see if my dusty old Sony stereo on the bookshelf still worked. It did, and that's when the rot set in. *Hunting the Wren* was one of the tracks and somehow it managed to get into my helmet and stay with me on and off for the duration of the whole End-to-End run.

'We'll hunt the wren,' said Richard to Robin
'We'll hunt the wren,' said Robin, a-bobbin'
'We'll hunt the wren,' said Jack o' the land
'We'll hunt the wren,' says everyone!'

At cruising speed H's exhaust-drum accompaniment seemed to fit perfectly. I am sure that my words are a free adaptation of the true original if there is one. Like so many folk songs, the writer seems to have been good old *Anon* and it has evolved over the years.

I stopped at the Stair Arms Hotel, Pathhead, which was welcoming and reasonably priced. H was found a berth in a storeroom at the back and I learned two things about Scotland. These are that the remote-control for the TV will not work and that the diet can be challenging if one is trying to avoid cholesterol. The 'healthy options' menu came with chips! (Tasted good though.) Next day I spent some time trying to think of another word in the English language, apart from Pathhead, proper nouns included, which contains two adjacent 'h's. It is surprising what can go on inside a helmet when you have to go so slowly and there is no Radio 4 to listen to.

Day's mileage: 165
Fuel: Richmond 2.55 litres, Jedburgh 4.5 litres

With young Aussies at Carter Bar

H can be a bit of a poser at times

Chapter 4

What's an H like to ride?

The Model H is a simple device. With five minutes of instruction and a ten-minute familiarisation run, any motorcyclist remotely worthy of the name, could ride an H almost anywhere with minimum damage to him / herself and at negligible risk to the public at large. Getting the best out of one for days on end, often in rain and wind over hilly roads is a different matter. I am still learning.

First start of the day from cold

Pump half a stroke of oil into the engine. Take bike off the stand and remember to clip stand up. With fuel cock closed and air and mixture (throttle) levers right off, operate valve-lifter and swing the engine over with the kick-start ten times to spread the oil around nicely. Open fuel cock and gently jiggle the end of a thin rod protruding from the top of the carburettor float chamber until fuel drips out. This process is graphically called 'tickling the carb'. Lift half-compression lever with toe of right boot. Set air and mixture levers to where experience has taught you they should be – usually somewhere near a third open for both, but no two bikes are alike. Set ignition lever to about the half-advanced point. Swing kick-start confidently. If there is no audience, the motor will cough into life immediately, whereupon deftly flick the half-compression lever down, let everything warm up a little while enjoying that lovely even exhaust beat, get astride, pull clutch, adjust the revs, select first gear and motor serenely away.

If there is an audience you will probably need several goes, flood the engine and have to change the plug before it finally agrees to come to life and you eventually ride off with the unclipped stand clanging merrily on the road behind you.

Starting when fairly warm

If you remembered to turn the fuel off when you stopped, no more than a caress of the valve-lifter with your left hand and a lazy prod at the kick-starter with the right foot will get her going. If you left the fuel on and the carb has flooded, then it is anyone's guess.

Starting from bloody hot

This can be a tricky one. Hs can get astonishingly hot and still exhibit few signs of distress. Mine has melted two pairs of over-trousers and inflicted radiation burns on my right calf. However, if you stop a very hot motor, heat can soak back to the carburettor and evaporate the fuel in the float chamber. If you are certain this is the case, you can operate the tickler vigorously and kick the motor over at once, sort of surprising it into life again. Or not! If in doubt, give it a five minute breather, change the plug (gingerly – it may melt gloves) and try again. Works for me.

On the road

A Triumph Model H does not accelerate; it gathers speed. Once it has gathered some, it stores it in a pair of vast flywheels. Anything less like a modern multi-cylinder bike is hard to imagine. Provided you can live with that concept, it is a delightful form of progression. The gearbox ratios are very wide, but you soon learn that the motor pulls well from low revs, so there is little to be gained from flogging it in the intermediate gears. I believe it is much better, whenever possible, to maintain a moderate, but steady speed in top, rather than trying to swap up and down the box to keep up with modern traffic. Apparently, a good H can reach over 55mph (90kph) on the level under ideal conditions, but I guess everything must be flapping around pretty wildly at that. I have had cars and vans check their speedos while following mine at its comfortable cruising speed and the result is always the same: 38mph. At that rate the motor doesn't feel stressed or vibrate excessively. Somehow all the internal clearances seem to be 'right in the middle'. I doubt if we exceeded this more than once or twice on the whole of the End-to-End run.

The bike corners adequately for its speed. Those big handlebars, the upright seating position and a front suspension system which guarantees that the wheelbase is constantly changing, do not exactly make for hairline steering, but considering her handicaps, H handles quite well.

On clear roads the only thing to worry about is keeping the oil supply going. All that is needed is a half-stroke of the manual oil pump on top of the tank every ten minutes. It is surprisingly easy to forget.

Braking

The Model H has braking devices on rear and front wheels. The rear one consists of a wedging block which is pressed into the belt rim. It is operated by a pedal high above the left footrest which cannot be reached without removing the foot from the rest. This is hardly ideal and braking with finesse unlikely. To add excitement in the wet, the wheel needs to rotate completely a couple of times to wipe the rim dry before the wedge takes effect. In any sort of crisis this can feel like a very long way indeed and one is tempted to give a panicky shove strong enough to lock the wheel the moment the rim does dry. Hard, 2½inch beaded-edge tyres skid easily under such provocation.

The front brake is a cycle-type stirrup pulling two small blocks onto the wheel-rim and worked by a puny inverted lever on the right handlebar. It plays little part in retardation and its presence must be treated as purely ceremonial. I have used it only occasionally, for holding the bike still while kick-starting on slight inclines. During the run, the nipple pulled off the cable on the third day and I didn't miss it at all. Overall, the best advice is always to ride an H as if there are no brakes and that way you won't be disappointed.

Signalling

In traffic on a vintage bike, looking behind and giving good clear hand signals is vital for self-preservation. Unfortunately, the ergonomics of the H don't make this easy. There is no mirror because I thought there was no chance of its being free enough of vibration to give a reliable image. Its lack means taking frequent looks behind and I often make these with a slightly exaggerated twist of the body which helps other drivers to see that a direction change is in the offing. I may be deluding myself about this, but it does seem to work. (Some time after the run I did find a mirror which yields a usable image and wish I had tried earlier.)

Naturally, there are no indicators fitted to the bike, so good old-fashioned hand signals come into their own. The problem is that when a hand is stuck out in the approved manner, it is not available for any other duties. Moreover, the remaining hand will be fully occupied with hanging on and steering. On a bike where the throttle, air, spark, clutch, gears, valve-lifter and horn are all hand operated, the potential difficulties are obvious. After a bit, you adjust to the concept that while you are indicating, everything else is going to have to wait, and ride accordingly. Thinking far ahead becomes an instinctive skill. All this, on top of the idiosyncratic braking performance, can make the rush-hour traffic experience uniquely challenging.

In the saddle

H was fitted with 'TT-Type' handlebars when I took her over. These were very wide, with a slight drop towards the ends. I understand they were the pattern specified for bikes destined for RFC despatch riders and no doubt they do allow great control of the front wheel on really rough or muddy roads. Ideal for Flanders, perhaps, but I hated them. I soon found that they put so much weight on the wrists and arms that a quarter-hour in the saddle was enough, and anyway, I didn't like the look of them either! I managed to get a pair of what Triumph's catalogue calls 'touring bars', which sweep up and back. I find them ideal. Now the riding position is very upright, but the hands remain fairly low, as if controlling a horse in an unflamboyant manner. The saddle is a Brooks, leather covered, with very little padding. Underneath it is marked '10/12', the weight range in stones for which its springs are designed. Fortunately I fit that range and find it very comfortable; it is large enough to move around on if the onset of numb-bum is detected. The springs are resilient but undamped, so that on road surfaces with close undulations a rhythmic bounce is easily induced. I have little doubt that this is a source of innocent entertainment for following drivers.

Altogether, H manages to be both simple and complex. Touring with her is a bit like travelling with an elderly aunt: she is capable of considerable activity, but demands constant consideration.

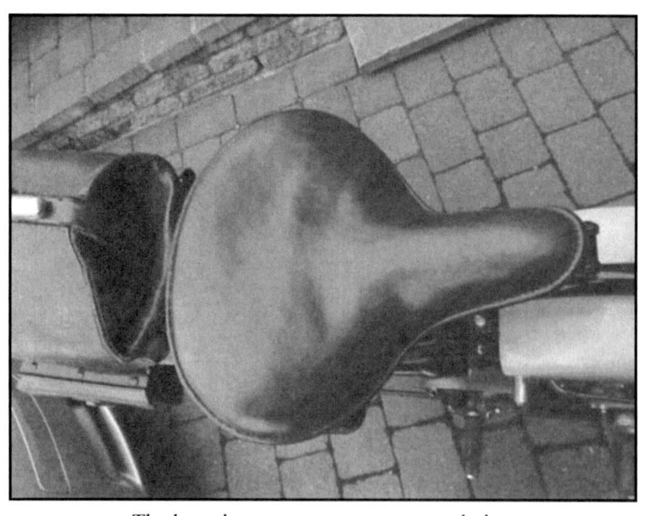

The luxurious passenger accommodation

Chapter 5

Big Bang at Crieff

Thursday 1 October

It had been a cold night and H's shed was open-fronted. Starting the bike with its SAE 50 oil in the crankcase was a laborious business. H grudgingly came to life after I changed the plug, but I didn't look forward to the prospect of even colder nights in the Highlands. Thick gummy oil was a far worse problem for motorcyclists in the early days and H was actually equipped with a device to overcome it: a priming cock. This is a small tap right on top of the cylinder into which a little neat petrol can be dribbled directly from an outlet controlled by a special knob on the tank. The petrol loosens up the thick oil on the cylinder walls and also provides a rich mixture to make cold-starting easy. I have always viewed priming cocks with deep suspicion on the basis that they provide a host of opportunities for gas to leak out of a hot engine and for raw petrol to drip over it. During all the years that H had started out from her nice warm garage at home, I had never felt any need to use the priming cock at all. I had even gone so far as to seal it permanently with a blob of solder. 'No need, with modern oils', I reasoned, 'and much less likelihood of leaks and fire...' Perhaps there is room for a re-think here.

Anyway, she fired up eventually and we were very soon doing battle with the morning traffic on the Edinburgh Ring Road, working towards the road bridge at South Queensferry.

The experience was enough to put me off the idea of returning via the same roads. H is not at her best amid a sea of articulated trucks bearing registration plates from across Europe and beyond, all of which can out-accelerate her at will. And, anyway, she is banned from Motorways because of her lack of lights. I had checked that the bridge took non-motorway traffic and devised a route accordingly. Unfortunately, I missed the planned road and sometime later found myself faced by the option of doing some complicated back-tracking or chancing about three miles on the M9. This was the stage when I started to become suspicious that the road numbers on my map bore only occasional similarity to those on the road signs. I could see the bloody bridge mocking me in the bright clear distance, so the M9 won, no problem. Having been conditioned by the Humber and Tilbury crossings, I feared I may have to stop and rummage for toll cash, so was delighted to find that the Forth Bridge is free. The morning was getting better and my route to the Highlands beckoned.

The suspension bridge I crossed surely gets the points for elegance, but it will never match the Forth Rail Bridge it parallels, for sheer visual drama. By its originality of design, the rail bridge is somehow timeless and it is hard to believe that this was the first-ever steel bridge on any scale, and is more than 30 years older than H.

Once north of the Forth, I was off arterial roads and into perfect old-motorcycle country. I meandered up through Dunfermline, Powmill and Gleneagles to Crieff, where I filled up at a handy garage at the top of the town. It was hilly going, but almost traffic-free. Saw a few other bikers, none of whom failed to wave. This was what I had hoped for: interesting riding through attractive countryside and no pressure or deadlines. Perfect!

Halfway along a straight climb, a few miles out of Crieff on the road to Aberfeldie, the even beat of H's engine stopped with a great clang of shocking abruptness. My immediate thought was 'That's it. Terminal!' I leaned the bike against the bank and expected to see a spreading pool of oil punctuated by shards of piston and crankcase. Instead, the only unusual sight was the spark-plug dangling on the end of the HT lead.

The plug I was using was a foreigner of East-European ancestry. It had served loyally in my other bike, a 1913 Triumph, and had been allowed on this trip as a spare. I had fitted it to H that morning, during the starting-up session. Now I gingerly swung the motor over with the plug out. Fine. Next, I rested the obviously very hot plug, on the head, inflicting severe burns on a rather nice leather glove in the process, and checked the spark … also fine. Half a bar of Kit-Kat later I re-fitted the plug, greatly relieved that there appeared to be no thread damage, and started tightening it down. It went so far and then resisted. I whipped it out again and noticed bright brass scrape marks on the valve cap where it had screwed in. I swapped it for a Champion which tightened down perfectly. Obviously, that morning, I had not noticed that a few thou of extra girth on the foreign plug had prevented it from seating properly and it had spent the morning gradually unscrewing. The force with which it had finally departed was impressive, putting a dent into the underside of the fuel tank and scaring the lights out of me. I was also impressed that the little wire clip which I use instead of a plug-cap had hung on gamely throughout all the excitement.

While I was stopped, an older biker flew past, then came back and checked I was OK. A little later, just as I was ready to set off again, a couple of younger bikers on Hondas were ready to stop, but I was able to wave them on. I am always grateful of offers of help, but sometimes, especially with an old bike like H, it can be a problem. I like to take my time deciding what may be wrong and try to be fairly systematic about putting it right. It sounds churlish, but in my experience that is much easier to do on your own! Now it is fine if the help comes from someone who is familiar with your model of bike, or at least those of similar age, but such folk are few and far between when it comes to something as venerable as H. Oh dear, that does make me sound mean, but it seems that the problem is far from a new one. According to a motorcyclist who is even older than I am, in the days before cellphones, Green Flag or Carole Nash Assistance, it used to be the custom to tie a white handkerchief to the offside handlebar if you were stopped by the road and would like help. Stopped and no hankie meant 'Having a sandwich', or 'Am just nipping behind the hedge for a pee'. It is a custom which it would be good to reintroduce.

I was soon on the road again after the plug drama, with H apparently unperturbed. Down a steep hill plastered with S-bend signs I met the two amiable young Honda riders, one of whom was retrieving his bike after an excursion into the scenery. No damage done, fortunately, but the scene took me back more than 50 years when I had the first of several unrehearsed field visits when cornering over-optimistically on my little Francis Barnett.

By afternoon, I had joined the A9 above Pitlochry and was making my way over the Grampians to Inverness via the Pass of Drumochter. Once or twice I took the old road, now often also designated a cycle route, for a few miles but hadn't yet grasped the idea that much of the A9 is paralleled by much quieter lanes, so I took my chances with the trucks most of the way. We covered the ground well, but in the mountains I really began to notice the drop in temperature and lusted after my long underpants which were still safely in the wardrobe at home. At Aviemore I stopped to buy some more, but failed. Those on offer were the high-tech variety which work on the principle of 'wicking away' any perspiration. I have experience of such garments when skiing and they do work very well indeed. Almost worth the eye-watering price. However, there is, as they say, a downside: after a day of even mild exertion they begin to smell pretty ripe - all that absorbed sweat concentrates the B.O. wonderfully. I was travelling light, so luxuries such as frequent changes of clothing were not available and I couldn't bank on overnight laundry. I passed up on the high-tech pants and decided to press on to Inverness, where I imagined there may be a wider choice.

As we motored out of the strip-development of Aviemore, the rain started. It didn't stop and I was wet and chilled by the time Inverness appeared. Out of the corner of my eye I spotted a Premier Inn sign and turned straight in. Bliss! The receptionist was charming and yes, a room was vacant. No garage, but H was allowed to be installed and sheeted up in a corner of the covered smoking area. I soon sank into a hot bath and let my mind roam back over the long day. As I started to doze off, the tap dripped with a regular rhythm. Yep, it was a slow version of *'We'll hunt the Wren ...'*.

Day's mileage: 200
Fuel: Crieff 4.46 litres, Newtonmore 3.45 litres

The spark plug that made a bid for freedom

Chapter 6

Groats

Friday 2 October

With porridge followed by fresh fruit salad for breakfast, I felt fuelled up ready for the ride along the east coast to the John o' Groats turnpoint. Needing to buy odds and ends and wine gums before setting off, I was directed to a large Tesco close to the Premier Inn. There I added women's leg-warmers and a pair of skiing gloves, each at a fiver a go, to my shopping basket and felt well satisfied. My black leather, specially-made-for-motorcycling gloves, had rather let me down in the rain the day before. Sodden, their Goretex membranes had managed to liberate themselves when I pulled the gloves off and had somehow migrated up into different fingers, forming the glove equivalent of apple-pie beds. There was no way of putting them on, so I had to resort to cutting the linings out altogether for the last part of the day. Needless to say, the colour ran too, so that I had signed in at the Inn with colliers' hands.

H started readily. I had mentioned the thick-oil problem to Ian Jennings when I had phoned him with a progress report the night before. 'Ah', he said 'You need to use the priming cock.' As that was inoperable, I now took the plug out and poured into the cylinder a spoonful of petrol which I had drawn out of the tank with a drinking straw. A couple of kicks and everything freed up nicely and she was raring to go. It was a bit of a rigmarole, though, fiddling around with the straw and removing the plug, and for the rest of the run I got away with simply turning the motor over a dozen times before attempting to make it fire. It worked fine, but another factor may just have been that I couldn't find any straight 50 grade oil when out on the road and had to compromise with 20/50 once my travelling supply had run out. This is OK, but the motor certainly seems to run cooler on long inclines with straight 50 in it.

I had also phoned Trevor Birkbeck, who, nobly and unasked, had somehow become my weather man. He is a great aviator, so can interpret synoptic charts with his eyes half closed. His information had been 100% accurate so far. 'Extreme weather, rain and gales forecast for the North of Scotland' he told me. I earnestly hoped he was wrong this time.

Even though H had started easily, I still had a job getting away from Inverness. First I was delayed in the car park by a well-meaning, but rather tedious gent who insisted on running through a comprehensive list of all the bikes his pals had owned in the forties and fifties. I don't think he had ever owned one himself. The list contained a number of implausible models such as Norton Thunderbird and Triumph Dominator, but I'm sure his heart was in the right place. Once rolling, I found that none of the places I had written out on my route the night before featured on any signposts, so I wrong-slotted a couple of times before sailing past Tesco from a new direction and eventually on to the A9 and north again.

Sea loch crossings are a great feature of the East Coast route. As the road leaves Inverness a handsome suspension bridge takes it high over the Moray Firth. Then it is on to the Cromarty bridge, which is much closer to the water; part causeway, part trestle. To the east all signs point to Nigg and its oil platforms which I could easily see. I had never been up here previously and these great water crossings were a fine surprise. Another thirty miles or so on the minor road through Invergordon and along the side of Nigg Bay brings the Dornoch Firth crossing, the most exposed of the lot. The weather was beginning to get a bit spirited and the waves seemed to be just below my left elbow as H moved about in the wind. 'Keep running, Love' I kept telling her, and she didn't let me down. The crossing is apparently about a kilometre, but it felt far, far longer.

It didn't need much sun assistance to make the water look silvery from a distance – the adjective Scotland's doggedly incompetent poet, William McGonagall, chose to describe the waters of the Tay at Dundee, into which North British Railway engine, number 224 had plunged in 1879, complete with carriages and passengers. I nursed a vague regret that my route did not take us across the Tay, if only because I had recently read that the engine involved in the disaster was recovered from the sea-bed and went back into service, to be known thereafter among Scottish railwaymen as 'The Diver'.

Approaching Dornoch, H had begun to weave a bit when trying to hold a straight line and it wasn't just down to the wind. It felt as though the steering head bearing adjustment had tightened up under the constant hammering it was getting. This is hard to check on an H without being able to rest the engine on a block so that the front wheel hangs free. About the only spanner I didn't have was one to fit the steering, so at Brora, well up the coast, I stopped at a garage and begged the loan of one. I slackened the nut off a couple of flats and hoped that would be about right, observing as I did it that rain was now falling steadily into the puddles on the forecourt. Never a good sign, that. The handling didn't improve either: holding a straight line was still a problem, but the bike was quite rideable provided I didn't demand hairline precision. The further I travelled to the north, the lighter the traffic became and I was comfortable with staying on the A9, not that there is really any option.

My research for the journey had been almost non-existent. Somehow I had got it in mind that the climb to be feared on the stretch above Inverness was the so-called 'Gateway to Caithness', the *Ord*, north of Helmsdale. It was raining when I got there. The climb was hard work for H, but we made it without much difficulty and I looked forward to an easy run along the coast for the rest of the day. I had reckoned without Berriedale ten miles further up the road. On my map this village looks innocuous, but Berriedale is at the bottom of a formidable incline from north or south. I guessed things may be beginning to get a bit challenging when it became obvious that the descent was steep enough to need middle gear, if not bottom, to keep the speed within reason, but the now-soaked belt was slipping wildly on the pulley as soon as I closed the throttle, even in top! With no engine braking available, all that was between H and the emergency run-out gravel traps thoughtfully provided for rogue lorries, was the rear brake block, which is also not at its best in the wet. Somehow we got down to the bottom while remaining upright, but I do recall sailing past a well-signposted car park on the way.

I knew I couldn't postpone the inevitable any longer. A belt-link would have to be removed. Right at the bottom I pulled off road to a quiet corner by the war memorial, heaved H onto her stand and got the tools out. Extracting a link is not really difficult, but it is inevitably a tricky business which involves crafty manipulation of a small screwdriver to prise the links over their connecting studs while crouching down in the dirt. There is a bit of a knack to it which takes time to learn. Few riders of belt-drive bikes have hands without a screwdriver scar or two. I was well into the process when a lady came out of a nearby cottage and told me, fairly politely, that the car park was some way up the hill and I was expected to use it. Although no longer lashing down, it was drizzling and I strained to retain my sense of humour. Anyway, after I had re-fitted the belt and she grasped that I was not feigning a breakdown, we parted on reasonably cordial terms. The rain had stopped while I was fixing the belt, so I gave it a good wipe with a rag with a bit of petrol on it to get it and the pulleys as clean as possible, and then let H loose on the climb up the north face of Berriedale. We made it, but it was touch-and-go all the way. I was fortunate to be able to detour into a large but empty lay-by on the outside of one of the steepest corners, effectively reducing the incline at that point and allowing H to gather a few extra revs for the final summit assault. Without the lay-by I would certainly have been reduced to pushing.

The signs on the climb announced 16%. OK, I am savvy enough to know that means seriously steep, but what does it mean *exactly*? Sixteen percent of what, precisely? Vertical? Horizontal? A right angle? These percentage signs which have taken over from the original system of '1 in 8', '1 in 10' and so on, seem stupid. The old method was self-explanatory and easily visualised.

I needed bottom gear on the climb out. Selecting this takes the right hand very close to H's cylinder head, and as soon as I went for it, the tip of the middle finger of my nice new Tesco ski glove melted. It spent the rest of the journey boldly sealed with an Elastoplast, the only use I found for my tiny first aid kit during the entire trip.

There was nothing half-hearted about the rain when I refuelled in Wick and rode the final 17 miles to John o' Groats. The landscapes up here become increasingly bleak and the occasional dwellings are built low to the ground, often looking as if they have sunk down into it to take cover during the last few centuries. Many are abandoned – a legacy of the Highland clearances, or possibly simply due to modern economic reality? A signpost indicated *Hill o' Many Stanes*. I wondered how that had distinguished it from any of the others. Only later did I discover that it is a prehistoric stone array and wished I had gone and had a look.

Approaching John o' Groats, I stopped at a hotel I saw just short of my goal, rather than risk floundering around searching for lodgings in the grim weather at dusk. After booking a room I rode on, to return later. The final half-mile of the road to the headland and little harbour is dead straight and slightly downhill. Aware that there was a degree of finality concerning the end of the road I braked in good time and hove-to in the rain-blasted car park. John o' Groats at last! I felt some satisfaction, but little elation; after all, I was only about a quarter of the way on my End-to-End odyssey.

Everything was the colour of dead elephants. And signs of human activity, zero. I took a photo of H in the rain and then a young Dutch couple appeared from the souvenir shop where they had bought tartan rugs, having sadly overestimated the temperature of the Caithness nights in their rental van. They were fascinated by H and happy to chat for long enough for her to cool down and the horizontal rain to drive into the magneto. They were schoolteachers who knew more about Scotland than I did and it was a shame that we did not meet in more clement weather – they were lovely company. After a photo or two I tried to start H, but she would have none of it. I only had to glance at the mag to have a fair idea of what the problem may be, and set about wheeling her to the cover of a small deserted shopping outlet. My new Dutch friends insisted on providing much of the motive power for this exercise. I wiped whatever I could, removed the pick-up, cleaned the slip-ring and she was running in no time. After that I made sure H was always parked in the lee if it was raining, and had no more loss of spark. Running on the road in rain is not a problem: the combination of engine heat plus H's generous front mudguard means that the magneto usually remains dry and obliging, and I have never had to resort to the common dodge of sealing it with Plasticine or silicone.

The hotel was less than a mile away and I was glad to get out of my soaking clothes and into a bath. H was berthed in a nice dry garage alongside the push-bikes of some other End-to-Enders whom I would meet in the bar that night.

Day's mileage: 128
Fuel: Dornoch 3.4 litres, Wick 2.54 litres

The ornamental front brake

Rear brake detail

Section of new belt & spare Links

A very welcome rainbow by the Hill o'Many Stanes

Duncansby Head lighthouse

John o'Groats after the storm

Mr Bosch's excellent magneto

and H's carburettor

Chapter 7

H, a brief biography

H was produced during the First World War at Triumph's factory in Coventry as part of military acquisition orders which resulted in at least 27,000 similar bikes being built – some estimates put the figure far higher. Unfortunately, the factory was completely destroyed in the Coventry blitz of 1940 and all the production records are lost. However, enough is known to be fairly sure that her engine is from 1917 and the frame from 1918. The gear-change mechanism is a little later, probably 1921, and far superior to the earlier version. The magneto is incorrect too, because I changed the original for the 1912 Bosch that is now on her. Before the war, the German Robert Bosch company supplied instruments of superb quality to much of the British motorcycle industry. Of course, as soon as hostilities were nicely under way the source of supply dried up and a number of British firms started making copies. They function well enough, but I don't think they match an original Bosch. I am not a purist and am not in the least bothered that H is a bit of a mongrel as long as she stays rideable and reliable.

The bike was very well restored in the late 1990s, by Glyn Udall, a Midlands enthusiast for all things motorcycle. In 2002 I swapped him a 1912 Triumph for it. Friends thought this was an eccentric thing to do on my behalf, because on the face of it the 1912 with its original registration number was worth rather more than the H, which has a later mass-issued number from the DVLA. For me it was a great deal, because I had found the earlier bike, which had only one gear, increasingly difficult to manage among modern traffic and, above all I like to *use* my old bikes! I knew the H, with its good three-speed gearbox and robust clutch, could handle almost any conditions, and so it has turned out to be.

Chapter 8

The H at war

Starting in 1915, the Triumph company supplied tens of thousands of their Model H to serve in the Great War. It is well known that they were liked by the servicemen who had to use them in battlefield conditions and gained a reputation for robustness – *Trusty Triumphs* indeed. My H is an ex-service machine and I have often wondered how it may have fared in the conflict, if indeed it ever went abroad, but will never know for sure. However, shortly after my run I had the great good fortune to hear about a local man, G H Foggitt, who served in France and Italy as a despatch rider for a Royal Engineers signals regiment. Mr Foggitt – Herbert to his friends – was an educated man with a wide interest in art and science. He was a trained architect. Fortunately, he also had sufficient disregard for authority to keep a diary throughout his service - something strictly against military law because of its potential value to the enemy in case of capture. I have been privileged to see this tiny journal and the story that emerges from its neat pencilled entries reveals a world in which the utterly mundane contrasts with the brutally bizarre on a daily basis. Unlike many whizz-bang memoirs, Herbert Foggitt's diary is a fascinating blend of observation, survival and duty. I have chosen only a few entries which specifically involve motorcycling. I am grateful to his son, Paul Foggitt, who transcribed the minutely written original, for permission to publish these extracts:

Thursday 7 September 1916:
during training at Houghton Regis camp, near Dunstable: (work) *Shops all day on Douglas, then on to BSA in aft. After tea, evg. fatigue with two motor lorries to Dunstable station to fetch packing cases of Triumph bikes. In camp rest of evening. Aeroplane came over camp about 7.30pm. Clifford Nunn cut hand in bread slicer. My vaccination almost quite well again. Saw my name on fatigue list for Hall guard on Friday evg.*

Training continued through autumn and winter and seems to have been very thorough. Drills and route marches were interspersed with much riding practice and lectures on maintenance and trouble-shooting.

Monday 13 November is typical:
Mess hut before breakfast - then relieved - fell in with squad. Route march and squad drill in morning. Aft.with fatigue party down to station - Breaking open crates and bringing Douglas bikes back to camp. Evg, Wesleyan Institute.

Training continued until February 15 1917, when Herbert and his Triumph were loaded onto the vessel *Archangel* and sailed to Le Havre and on up the Seine to Rouen. The next month was spent behind the lines around Abbeville and St Pol, and doesn't sound to have been very demanding. However, April 1917 was a vile month, with frequent snow.

Thursday 12 April:
Off at 4am to 3rd Army. Rode with Binder as far as Hesdin. Snowing on Hesdin-St Pol road - a blizzard. Had to walk

halfway on bye-road to tanks. Breakfast and dinner at DR's billet. Return journey at 4pm. Arr GHQ 5:40. Evg. Shaved at widow Meron's.

Punctures feature frequently in the diary, as do belt-slippages and broken footrests, but Foggitt always seemed to manage to complete his journeys. The routes were fairly well established and the DRs often travelled in pairs. Dead horses and disabled tanks are commented upon, as well as nearby bombardments and vast and prolonged explosions in an ammunition dump. One day, near Bapaume, he attempted to pick up a woollen glove, only to discover that it was still on the hand of an ill-buried corpse.

The routine continues through the summer, but reference to nearby bombardment becomes increasingly frequent.

Monday 23 July:
finds him on a hilltop at Cassell watching the action:
Heavy bombardment all along front ... Saw 16 searchlights and 16 observation balloons. Gunfire - liquid fire - aeroplanes – starshells - shrapnel - AA guns - machine guns. 4am set off back - good run to GHQ. Breakfast. Paraded 8-30 medical hut with gunners. Saw doctor about tooth needed filling ...

The Model H continued to run well, as the entry for Sunday 2 September shows:
To Albert(ville) with Cpl May. Good run through ... rode via Bray, Cappy, Villers Carbonnel - Peronne - Babaume ... good ride ... did 170 miles in all. Bed soon.

Eventually the hard use took its toll on the bike. In September he fitted a new gearbox and a front fork spring, attended repeatedly to the magneto and was plagued by punctures. Then the engine began to complain.

Herbert Foggit photographed in France during September 1917. His Machine is almost identical to *H.* He carries a spare drive-belt wrapped around the front forks and the container clipped below the toolbox on the rear carrier will probably hold a spare inner-tube

Chapter 9

Two days to Dalwhinnie

Saturday and Sunday 3-4 October

The pedal cyclists in the hotel had ridden up from Land's End, taking two weeks, and were going to their homes on the train from Thurso tomorrow. Their timing had been almost perfect, a high-pressure system having been established over the British Isles for most of late September. They all had healthy tans. They were all in great good humour at having completed their runs and didn't mind having got a bit damp during the last few miles when the cold front overtook them. That was the same front that I had managed to catch up and get tangled with for the last day and a half. It is a long hilly ride from Land's End and pedalling it must be a hell of a slog. I didn't begrudge them their fine weather. I also worked out that Thurso was downwind from here, so they would get there pretty sharpish.

There was a TV in my room, with the statutory non-functioning remote control. The forecast for northern Scotland was exactly what Trevor had predicted. I looked out of the window to check and in the light of the hotel could see only a plastic bag impaled on a barbed-wire fence being systematically shredded by the wind as it blew out horizontally. By morning only half the bag's handle was left, still horizontal, but the rain was merely intermittent. 'Oh, well' I thought, 'I'll give it a couple of hours and see if the sky lightens'. It didn't and so I booked in for another night.

By mid afternoon I had read more Dan Brown than can be good for anyone, so during what appeared to be a lull I went down to the harbour on foot as a bit of light relief. I bought postcards and stamps at the souvenir shop; there weren't many other signs of life and I got the impression that the season for tripper's coaches was well and truly over. I took pictures of the waves breaking over the harbour and set off back up the incline whereupon the breeze picked up to the extent that it became difficult to stay on the pavement. That gave me the comfort of knowing that I had made a good decision not to leave today – H would have been all over the road.

In the garage I took the opportunity to give the bike a good going-over. I managed to find an old paint tin on which I gingerly perched her so that the front wheel was off the ground and I could see what the problem was with her steering. It was soon obvious that I had guessed wrongly about the tightness and that it was all too slack. I did what I could to tighten it, but the tools at my disposal were not ideal and trying to drift the nut around using a six-inch nail and a seven pound sledge-hammer (yes, really) was a primitive business. That made some improvement. I finished off by running spanners over most of the nuts, oiling the primary chain and putting the old girl away 'till morning.

It wasn't raining as I left the hotel on Sunday morning – well, not proper rain, just drizzle and that doesn't count at these latitudes. I rode down to the harbour for an extra photo of H before we went south. It was still deserted. Then on to Duncansby Head lighthouse, a couple of miles away.

Not only did I want to take a look at the rock stacks in the sea there, but I would be able to silence people who, when hearing of trips to John o' Groats, delight in saying ' It's not the farthest point, you know, that's Duncansby Head – the farthest from Lands End!'
Been there, seen it.

Proper rain was threatening. A signpost pointed along a lumpy footpath to 'Stacks ¾ m'. I didn't fancy a yomp in my motorcycle boots, so H and I gave the stacks a miss and drove away for Wick and all points south. I tried to pretend that the belt hadn't shown signs of slip on the small hill on the way back to the main road, but I knew it had.

Now the sky really was seriously black ahead of me. I got my oversuit on just in time and splashed on, the belt slipping almost continuously and some footing needed to breast even modest inclines. We were still up in very exposed countryside and any shelter would have been welcome. The best I could find was a railway bridge near the entrance of a bleak-looking sort of quarry site. Almost too late – blame the rain on my glasses - I found it was gated off and struggled out up the access slope again. Decidedly dispirited, I was about to move on as best I could when a Landrover appeared at a gate on the other side of the road. The driver let me in and showed me another bridge which I could use. I don't think he had seen me from afar – I was just dead lucky. I put my old spare belt on and hoped for the best.

The thing about a spell in the rain on an old motorbike is that it is so lovely when it stops. It stopped, and near the Hill o' Many Stanes I parked H to take a photo of her framed by a rainbow. Then we kept going down the coast. On the way up I had been very occupied with reaching the top. Now I could relax and enjoy the often-spectacular views. Berriedale was a struggle again, but at least I knew what we were in for and it wasn't as bad as on the outward trip. It was still very windy and I was a bit anxious about crossing the bridge over the Dornoch Firth, but it wasn't a problem. Just for a change, I didn't take the Cromarty crossing, but went on to Inverness via Dingwall.

On the flatter parts of the coast road H's beat had settled as usual and a familiar tune began to creep into my helmet again. … *We'll hunt the wren, said Jack o' the land, We'll hunt the wren said ev-er-y one!* Oh dear.

Inverness was drenched in sunlight, with a match in full flow at the Caledonian Thistle stadium as H thumped past on the A9. I doubt if any of the fans noticed us.

My route at this stage was the reverse of my way up, but I tried to leave the A9 more and take the old minor roads whenever possible. This was great and I travelled almost traffic-free. The snow line was clear as a knife along the Cairngorms and Grampians, and I had a cold ride through Boat of Garten, Alvie and Kingussie to Dalwhinnie, which was reached at the end of a long empty stretch. It had been a hard day of riding and I was pleased to find the Inn. H was parked around the back and I moved in. Pausing only to reassure myself that the Scottish tradition of inoperative TV remote controls was being upheld (it was), I made for the bar and dinner. In all the days I had been in Scotland I had not so much as smelt a whisky. Now, I planned to correct that!

With a sense of keen anticipation, I took a bar stool in front of a display of the distillers' art: there were rare single malts, affordable single malts and perfectly acceptable blends. There were whiskies I had heard of and whiskies whose names I am convinced were invented only to confuse the English. Any one of them would do fine.
"I'm sorry, sir, I can't serve you a drink."
'Hell, I thought, it's Sunday and I'm not even a Christian. This is victimisation!'

It wasn't because it was Sunday and it wasn't a bad joke. Licence withdrawn for an undisclosed reason, so no booze. Because I was a resident I was allowed a 'complimentary' lager with my meal and had to settle for that. I can't remember what I ate – my brain is still full of that panorama of unattainable scotches.

I coaxed the TV to show me the news. Apparently the skiing had been good, with the Cairngorm lifts open for the first time this season.

Day's mileage: 190
Fuel: Brora 3.94 Litres, Carrbridge 3.79 Litres

A miscellany of H's parts

An audible warning of approach

A genuine Brammer belt - impossible to find, so kept for special occasions

The ornamental front brake

Spring on forks and belt in case it should break

Half-compression lever open for starting……And closed to run

Chapter 10

Long ago

The route between the extremities of the British mainland has held a fascination for travellers since Victorian days, if not before. The beginnings are understandably hazy, but reliable pedal-cycle records go back to 1888, so it is no surprise that by the early 1900s motorcyclists were completing the Land's End - John o' Groats route and vice-versa. Naturally, as soon as a time was publicised it became the time to beat!

The years 1901 to 1910 can now be seen as the golden days of End-to-End record chasing, although at the time they saw more than their share of anguish and disaster. I doubt if any of today's travellers can imagine how difficult the route must have been. Away from any town the road surface was, if you were lucky, 'unbound macadam' – in other words stones and gravel compacted by a horse-drawn roller. This was astonishingly dusty when dry and proportionately slippery and muddy when wet. If you were not lucky, the road could be little better than a sheep track and north of Inverness it tended to disappear altogether in places. In the towns there would probably be cobble-stoned surfaces, liberally interlaced with tram lines. A variation may have been wood-block paving, smooth and quiet when dry but like ice when damp. There were no bridges across the three main sea-loch crossings, so the choice was between detours of many miles on muddy tracks or a ferry propelled by sail or oars.

The ferries didn't operate according to a timetable, but merely responded to demand. If, when the traveller turned up the boat was on the opposite shore, the advice was to raise a flag. A similar service after dark involved the lighting of a bonfire.

At least the traffic would have been sparse, but horses featured in 99% of it so there must have been a degree of unpredictability and a glut of horseshoe-nails on the surface. Nobody needed a driving licence then, and clear rules of the road had not been established.

The first record of motorcycling from End-to-End is of Hubert Egerton on a French Werner in 1901. This was essentially a pedal cycle with a clip-on motor mounted in front of the steering head and driving the front wheel via a rawhide belt. The pioneer motorcycle journalist the Rev Basil H Davies, who wrote under the pen-name of *Ixion*, describes this top-heavy model as 'The champion skidder of all time' in his wonderful book *Motor Cycle Cavalcade* (1950). He goes on to say 'I still remember trying to keep it vertical along the Euston Road one wet November day, when the roadway was smeared with a terrible greenish paste compounded of pulverised horse dung, rainwater and all the assorted filth of an imperfectly scavenged city'.

I have seen a lovely photo of Hubert Egerton posing at the start of his run, wearing a business suit and a straw boater. Bearing in mind that he is about to spend at least three or four days directly behind a primitive engine with total-loss oiling and a front wheel which is completely devoid of any mudguarding, I am prepared to bet he looked a lot less jaunty at the other end. I don't know how long Hubert took, but in 1902, E H Arnott needed only 65 hr 45 min on his 'new' Werner from Land's End to John o' Groats. The new Werner was still really a motorised pedal cycle, but the engine was now fitted at the bottom of the frame, where virtually all motorcycle engines have remained to this day.

When these Werner riders made their attempts, the national speed limit was a mere 12 mph. It was raised to a giddy 20mph in 1903. Tarmac for surfacing roads was not patented until April 1902, so it is safe to say that none of their riding was done on tarred roads. On my ride in 2009, *all* of it was on tarmac!

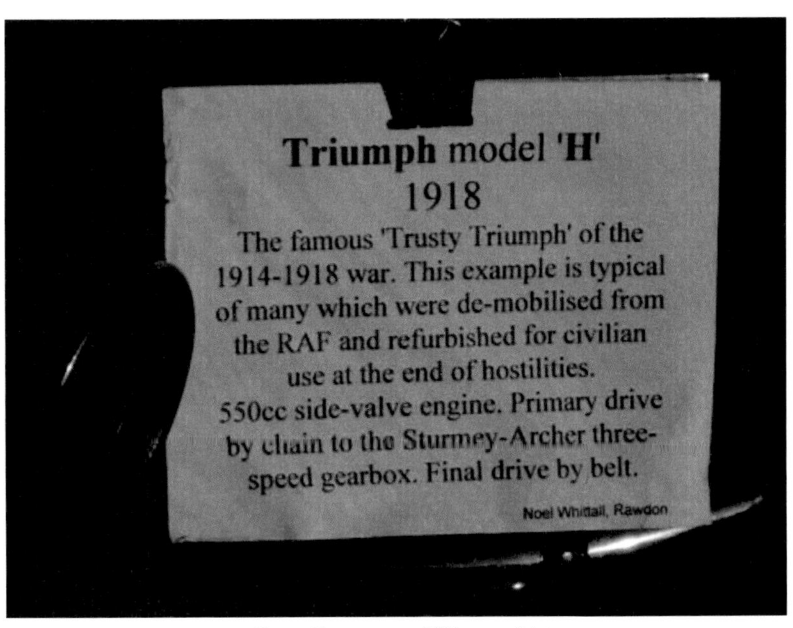

Revealing some of H's past history

More of H's important bits

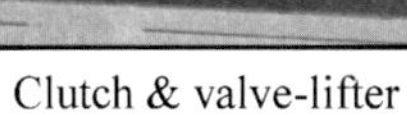

Clutch & valve-lifter

Gearbox end

The all-important manual oil pump

The rear brake

Chapter 11

Not the best of days

Monday 5 October

I got away from Dalwhinnie in pleasant weather after a long interrogation by an amazed and amused Swedish couple. He really had been a biker and knew his stuff – not at all like some of the folk I met. It made delaying my start by a few minutes into a pleasure. After some tough miles on the A9, I could turn off onto the old road for a lovely easy run through Blair Atholl and Aberfeldy. This is whisky country in a big way and I was tempted to stop at the Dewar's distillery to take a photo of H posed alongside a steam tank loco which they have parked outside. I pulled in, but it all looked very 'out of season' and I didn't feel very sociable, so I rode on to Amulree. We had no trouble with the hefty climb out of town and were soon passing the site of my plug blow-out of a few days earlier and on the way to Crieff. H was going beautifully but I was feeling a bit part-worn. A stomach ache nagged at me on and off. I simply thought I must have been sitting awkwardly, and certainly when I shifted around on the saddle it seemed to go away for a bit. On the way out of town, I pulled in to the Stuart Glass shop which had the sort of restaurant I like when I have to park H: big glass windows where I can keep an eye on her. I felt that I needed to eat, yet had little appetite. I managed to choke down a 'toastie' – ham and cheese – but it may as well have been Polyfilla. Lots of tourists here, with lots of questions too.

Travelling south from Crieff there are basically three choices: east, which involves Edinburgh, west, which involves Glasgow, or wriggling down the middle through a string of small towns which are familiar to me solely from Saturday night football results. I decided to do the wriggle and after passing through the charismatically named *Yetts o' Muckheart,* was making for the Kincardine Bridge. As soon as I reached the main road, instead of settling into the expected *Hunting the Wren* beat, H began to cough a bit and lose power. Eventually, just a few miles from the bridge I had to pull off into a farm road and investigate. After a couple of plug changes and a lot of grovelling around, I found that the magneto points were almost closed. Re-setting them did the trick, but altogether, I reckon I lost the best part of an hour by the time I had got the bike loaded up again and running properly. I should have diagnosed the problem much quicker, but I wasn't feeling bright at all at this stage. I don't remember the bridge very well and the toil of trying to escape the clutches of the M9 and M876 signposting regime is with me to this day. On my map it looked simple, but few of the road numbers I needed ever appeared. It all seemed to take a long time and by the time I had done three laps of Airdrie before being told 'Turn left at the Gala Bingo and go straight on' I was very tired, but at least I was going south. I had vaguely hoped to make Carlisle that night, but the rush hour was warming up nicely and I knew this was absurdly optimistic. I settled for Lanark, just as the rain started.

I guess I didn't get off to the best possible start at the guest house when I appeared at the front door with my helmet still on and the charming woman who ran the place immediately assumed that I was a police motorcyclist bearing either grim news or a summons. Once we had put that right, I set about finding a berth for H behind the house. With her just about settled I suddenly realised that the occasional stomach pains I had experienced through the day were warnings of sinister activity within my digestive system. I needed a toilet now! No, not at the top of the stairs in a minute or two. NOW! My mind being elsewhere, I forgot to screw down H's fuel cock.

My knock on the back door brought the Master of the House, who, fortunately, showed a sharp and commendable response to my gabbled request and pointed soundlessly to a bathroom just across the hallway. I hurled myself at it like a bow-legged whippet. My situation was not aided by the fact that under my leather jeans I had both male underpants and female leg-warmers – no recipe for speed. Disaster was averted, but it had been a photo-finish. I felt I had done little to endear myself to my host but the rest of my stay went well enough. It's amazing what a hot bath and an industrial dose of Diocalm can achieve.

Day's mileage: 148
Fuel: Pitlochry 3.03 litres, Slamannan 1.61 litres

The obligatory 'First and Last House' shot at Gretna Green

H spending a comfortable night at the Whoop Hall Inn,
courtesy of Mr Boleta, the landlord

Chapter 12

Shap and that

Tuesday 6 October

I took my time before leaving next morning – I didn't want to experience one of those toilet-panic moments once I was under way and layered up in my foul-weather gear. I ambled down into the town and hunted out the Tesco to stock up on Diocalm and Rennies, just in case. Also, my wine gum stocks were perilously low. Tesco had what I needed, but wasn't up to Inverness standards. From there the high street was at the end of *Bull Close*, a tiny lane through which the village bull was admitted in mediaeval times. In most of England this would be called an alley and around my Yorkshire home they are ginnels or snickets. I would learn another regional word before I left Lanark: *smirr*. This is an excellent expression to describe that grade of drizzle which is so fine that you don't notice it until it is too late. It is a curious form of precipitation, so subtle that you can't tell if it is falling down or rising up from the ground. It is simply there, yet quite different from its cousins, mist and low cloud.

I had lost my small tarpaulin (think I had forgotten to strap it on the carrier again after an oversuit-donning stop) and my search for a replacement took me to Jack's Hardware store, which should be declared a national treasure. Not only did the stock seem inexhaustible, but the friendly staff were determined that their customers got exactly what they were looking for.

Lanark was cocooned in smirr as I prepared H for the off. I spent some time deciding whether it was rain starting, in which case the oversuit would be needed, or rain stopping, so I could go without. I played safe, which turned out to be the right choice. I see that my notebook simply starts with 'Tuesday October 6 The wet day'.

H smelled suspiciously of petrol and the float bowl was already full when I started her up and I knew that some fuel had seeped out of the tank overnight. Bugger. There was still enough to get me down the road, so we chugged out of Lanark, bound for the old A6, Carlisle and Penrith. Somewhere along here I noticed that the throttle lever was waggling about more than usual. A closer look showed that it had fractured through metal fatigue and was remaining in place thanks only to the dogged loyalty of a tiny rivet. Fortunately there was an easy fix: I swapped the air and throttle cables over, so that now the air lever controlled the throttle and vice versa. I fixed a cable-tie around the broken lever so that it wouldn't be lost completely if the minute rivet stopped hanging on. I was able to set the air reasonably well by careful use of the damaged lever and drive almost normally using what had been the air lever as the throttle. Sorted.

H was in top form in spite of increasingly wet weather and problems finding the almost-deserted minor roads which parallel the M74 and M6. Her engine was beating as steadily as the rain, but I was well wrapped up and we enjoyed apparently racing the trucks as they drove the nearby motorway, sometimes sufficiently close to get a wave from a driver. We were always generous enough to let them win. My stomach felt reasonably settled too, although I didn't dare risk a fart until I was well past Carlisle. I reckoned I had last ridden this road in 1973, on my then almost-new BMW, and knew that there were hills to come. We made great progress through Abington and Beattock to Lockerbie and Gretna Green, where I stopped for the obligatory photo and then detoured to Longtown. Since my '73 visit, Gretna seemed to have metamorphosed into one large factory outlet.

I had expected Beattock to be hard, due to old W H Auden again. His *Night Mail*, the poem accompanying the Royal Mail's famous 1936 documentary film, opens:

This is the Night Mail crossing the border,
Bringing the cheque and the postal order,
letters for the rich, letters for the poor,
the shop at the corner and the girl next door.
Pulling up Beattock, a steady climb:
The gradient's against her, but she's on time.

Auden's verse fits Benjamin Britten's music and the beat of the steam engine perfectly on the film. I could fit it to H's syncopated tappets and underlying exhaust beat equally well, but after a few miles *Hunting the Wren* replaced it and we were back to normal! After all that, Beattock was an easy climb and we had no trouble. Just Shap to come … after the traffic knots and vague signposting in Carlisle and Penrith, that is.

A little further south, I stopped for a coffee at a petrol station. It is my opinion that filling station coffee tends to represent the apex of the cynical art of marketing. Relatively speaking, the coffee itself is cheap, so they make you buy a far larger portion than you had in mind to maximise the turnover and hopefully, leave you imagining that you are getting something like value. You choose the cheapest because they don't offer 'small' and get a 'regular' which is almost the size of a young bucket. Then you see they have printed a sort of sermon on the cardboard cup informing you that this is not just a hot drink, but part of 'Your Lifetime Coffee Experience' or buzzwords to that effect and assuring the drinker how dedicated and ethical the company is. Quel load de bollocks!

The climb up Shap Fell is very long, but not too steep and we needed second gear only briefly. It is the exposure and air of desolation which are special. We were almost alone on the road. This is no place to break down, especially in horizontal rain. My map says it is eighteen miles from Penrith to Tebay via Shap and I willed H on for every inch. She didn't fail me and there was a golden moment when, just as I realised the climbing was over, sunlight briefly lit the route to Kendal. Unfortunately the moment was transitory and I had the usual struggle reading a sodden map in the rain while trying to find the back route out of town. I was making for Kirkby Lonsdale, which is just off the A65, the road which, in about a further fifty miles, runs past the end of my street. Psychologically, I would feel almost home when I got to the A65.

Kirkby Lonsdale was like a ghost town when I rode in. Apart from a couple of dispirited teenagers in the square, there was no sign of life. The main hotel seemed to be closed and I didn't pass any appealing-looking B & Bs. I began to wish I had stopped in Kendal but had little choice other than pressing on and hoping for the best. Fortunately, the best soon turned up in the form of the Whoop Hall Inn, right at the side of the main road. I parked H and with a fair degree of trepidation squelched up to the reception desk, a pool forming on the Axminster as I stood there. Yes, they had a room, the price was more than fair, and yes, H could be parked under cover.

Out of my wet clothes, I asked exactly where H would go. “Here, inside, I show you” said Mr Boleta, the proprietor. We went down a carpeted corridor, on the way, I presumed, to a back door and an outhouse. But he stopped after a few paces. “In here.” He opened the door to the ballroom. “In here!”

I protested. 'She's wet, she's dirty. She can't come in here.'

“I am the boss and I say she can!”

I couldn't argue. After reaching an agreement that at least we put some cardboard down to protect the floor, H was wheeled in and spent the night in state.

Mr Boleta's hospitality was typical of the hotel. The crab linguini for dinner was delicious, the house red excellent and every member of the staff welcoming. In the bar I got into conversation with Alan, a motor trade representative who came from Faversham in Kent. He was fascinated by H. He mentioned a friend whom he referred to as Dick, who, he

said, 'Has this type of thing and would be very interested'.
“Not Richard Mummery?” I asked.
That was the man, and I was able to tell Alan that only a month previously I had been over in Belgium with the very same Richard, who had been riding another Model H!

Day's mileage:140
Fuel: Abington 4.39 litres, Penrith 2.74 litres

Chapter 13

Halfway

Wednesday 7 October

I awoke to a world of mist through my bedroom window and thought 'Oh, hell, not again...'

I needn't have worried. The mist was generated by my Belstaff jacket which had been steaming gently over the radiator thanks to its advanced moisture-retaining qualities. Behind it was blue sky and a patina of frost on the fields and car roofs. The Whoop Hall is just in Yorkshire and the country looked wonderful.

H and I rode home together through a perfect clear morning. There was another five mile spell of Lancashire, where a spike of that county rather curiously sticks up into North Yorkshire, almost reaching the foot of Whernside, which with its flat-top peaked neighbour, Ingleborough, dominates the northern side of the A65 here. After riding through the village of Ingleton, we left the main road to climb up over Buckhaw Brow and down through Settle. Now by-passed along with Settle, Buckhaw used to be a feared obstacle for laden family cars from industrial West Yorkshire bound for holidays in Morecambe, Blackpool or the Lake District. Today H made light work of it.

With an overnight stop at home in prospect, the pressure was off and I called to cadge a cup of tea with Kate, an artist friend in Gargrave. For the previous week I had just kept going, knowing that if I spent much time with visits or at tourist attractions I would never achieve my prime objective. Now it was a bit different. I was almost back on home turf and it was great to enjoy a bit of company and chat in Kate's kitchen.

The run through Skipton was easy and soon we were in the genteel streets of Ilkley, where my old friend Scott lives. I phoned him from the town centre. Yes, he was in. Yes, we could have lunch together and, as a bonus, another pal, Pete, was there too. Perfect. We had all got together almost twenty years ago through an interest in flying paragliders. Neither Scott nor Pete knew of my trip, so my arriving on the H was unexpected. They are both motorcyclists and know me very well, so it wasn't too much of a surprise. Lunch was simple but very jovial and I had to remind myself that I was only about halfway on my journey. It would have been easy to get into a premature spirit of celebration!

Leaving Scott's house, H began coughing and spluttering and I thought I was going to have to attend to plug or magneto before I reached home. Just in time I realised that the problem was me. I had relaxed so much (no, it had been a teetotal lunch if you're thinking what I imagine you are thinking) that I had forgotten that the air lever was now the throttle. I made the necessary mental adjustment and we positively glided the last ten miles to my home.

51 miles

Chapter 14

Pit stop

I had planned my arrival quite carefully. H and I rolled up to my house on the afternoon of Wednesday 7 October, almost eight days to the hour since we had left. I produced the electronic garage door key from my jacket pocket, awarding myself a couple of extra points for having had the foresight to take it with me so we could ride straight in. With H taken care of, I climbed the front steps, fell over the accumulated mail behind the door, left the light flashing on the answering machine, ignored my computer, took a beer from the fridge and went to wallow in a hot bath while reading the newspaper which I had bought on the way home. That, I thought, was a golden example of thinking ahead. My plan would have been flawless had not the hot water system lost its pressure while I was away, so I shortly found myself stark naked with only cold water on tap. I had to pad down to the garage in a dressing gown to get it fired up again. Took the edge off things a bit.

Ian Jennings called on Thursday morning and together we serviced the bike. There was surprisingly little to do, the only tricky job was adjusting the steering head properly. My John o' Groats botching had been fairly successful, but there was room for improvement. We soon had the handlebars off and could see exactly why the bearings didn't seem to be seating properly. After a bit of juggling and improvising a spanner from a G-clamp, Ian got them moving smoothly with no slack. He found some excessive play in the nut holding the fork spring in place too and with that nipped up, the steering was as good as new. It seems that at some time in the dim past a non-standard collar had been fitted which was reluctant to be tightened correctly. That sort of thing is very common on machines as old as H and some remarkable bodges sometimes emerge during a restoration. Curiously, it is easier to obtain many replacement parts now than it was forty or fifty years ago. The vintage and veteran movement has grown to the extent that there are a number of specialists such as Ian who can supply virtually anything needed for bikes which may be a century old.

The broken throttle lever problem was solved by removing the entire unit and replacing it with an identical one from my 1913 Triumph. That was a five-minute job and the broken part can be properly repaired over the winter.

The oil tank was filled with straight 50 oil again and a bit more 80/90 grade went into the gearbox. Topping up the gearbox has to be done with restraint, as any surplus very quickly escapes down the shaft to the belt pulley, where it continues with its job of lubrication. Unfortunately, that is about the last thing the belt needs.

The wheels were checked and apart from slight adjustment of the front wheel bearings, no attention was required. I was impressed by that, because loose or broken spokes are not unknown. Indeed, I had needed a very short-notice re-tensioning of the front wheel to get H through her MOT test only a week or so before my ride. I also made a careful check for signs of the tyres moving on the rims.

H uses old-fashioned 'beaded-edge' tyres. These were the standard type until the mid-1920s when the modern wired-edge covers were introduced. The beaded ones have no reinforcing wires and rely for fit on the edges of the rim engaging with moulded grooves in the tyre walls. They work fine, but unless they are run fairly hard, can tend to creep and eventually pull the valves out of the inner tubes. I run mine at around 40 to 45psi and rarely have any trouble, although as you can probably imagine, it hardly results in a cushioned boulevard ride.

While in the warm and dry I also took the opportunity to change about half a dozen of the belt links which were looking a bit out of sorts. When removing or replacing them 'in the field' (and usually in the rain) I had not always been scrupulous in making sure that the studs were absolutely perfectly set above the top of each link, so a few were beginning to burrow down into the layers of fabric and I felt they needed replacing. That is easier said than done, as four studs pass through each link and my fingers were aching before the end of the task. I was glad when I was eventually able to flip the belt back over its pulley-rim and leave H for the night. By now I thought I knew enough about belt tension to guess it correctly without going for a trial run.

I made a shopping expedition on the bus into Leeds for yet another pair of gloves and spent the evening clearing my post. I also made a few changes to the small amount of gear I carried with me. I added a pair of cotton trousers, so I didn't have to go to hotel dining rooms in my leathers. I put a few more pairs of latex gloves in the toolboxes to use when mechanicing or belt adjusting and as a result had cleanish hands for the rest of the run. I slung out the half-read Dan Brown because there is only so much breathless implausibility a man can take. I replaced the book with a biography of Bernard Madoff, the Wall Street financial criminal who stole billions. He had Manhattan apartments, houses in Florida and the French Riviera, yachts and limousines galore and now he is about my age and in gaol for the rest of his days while I am having the time of my life cruising around the country as free as a bird on an ancient motorcycle. From my perspective it is a feel-good read!

I was keen to get under way again, but there didn't seem much point in setting off for at most an hour of riding, so I had a second night in my own bed.

0 miles
Leeds 4.5 litres

Chapter 15

Away again

Friday 9 October

I set off confidently up my street, which is fairly steep and the belt slipped almost immediately. I had guessed wrongly last night. I pressed on for a mile or two, but realised that further attention was essential, so I decided to make a small deviation and call at Ian's house in Bradford. I was sorry that I hadn't got under way cleanly and was eager to get the belt fixed and then pile on the miles. The Leeds-Liverpool canal lies between my house and Ian's, and for the first time I can remember, the swing bridge on the back road I had chosen was closed in favour of boat traffic. Normally I enjoy watching the canal, but today I could have done without the delay. Indeterminate waits like this always pose the dilemma of whether to stop the motor or not: leave it and it will get hot and bothered; stop and it may be reluctant to start again, with a string of cars waiting behind. This time I kept her running and soon enough we were at Ian's. This was an excellent ploy, because he kindly took a link out while I enjoyed a cup of tea.

Just after nine, with the rush-hour thinning, I was on my way again, through thc middle of Bradford and on out to Huddersfield and the Summer Wine town of Holmfirth. I know these roads well and made good time until stopped by roadwork traffic lights on a steep incline leaving Holme Bridge. This is a little pig of a climb which would have been easy if we had been allowed a run at it, but no chance. I had a job getting away from a dead stop and had to leg it quite hard. Normally I wouldn't have been too worried by this, but I knew that an even bigger test was to follow: Holme Moss, which climbs to more than 1700ft (520m). In the early 1960s I had come this way frequently when I was involved with road-testing brake linings for the Mintex company. The next part of my trip to Land's End would follow one of the regular evaluation routes we used.

The day was grey and wind howled over the dry-stone wall by which I was glad to shelter while extracting yet another link on the way up. I had not bargained for how much the new links needed to bed in until the angles of their studs matched those of the rest of the belt. At least it was not raining.

This stretch, high in the Pennines, really does feel like the backbone of England. After the long drop from the Moss, nursing my precious brake and taking my time with the engine chuffing in second gear on the steep bits, the route took me across Woodhead Reservoir then up over the tops again via the Devil's Elbow to Glossop and the Peak District. Through Glossop, Chapel en le Frith and then Buxton before picking up the Ashbourne road with its panoramic views across the Peaks. H relished the cool weather and was beating to *Hunting the Wren* as usual whenever the road flattened out.

Between Chapel and Buxton the road runs straight through Dove Holes, a village whose economy was based on local quarries and which, to be fair, does not exude any particular aura of charm, but a certain memory still makes me chuckle whenever I pass through. In my Mintex days, Dove Holes was a dreary stretch of 30mph in the middle of exhilarating miles of unlimited speed. Remember, that was back in the 1960s, when a black diagonal on a white disc really did mean 'no limit' – none of your weedy 70 mph then. One day, our most senior engineer, Lionel, a passionate pipe smoker, was caught in a speed trap set in Dove Holes and later suitably fined. From then on he made a ritual of emptying his ashtray every time he passed through the village, albeit at a steady 30 mph! Seemed a bit unfair to me, but it went unremarked because in every other possible way Lionel was the ultimate gentleman.

A few miles further on I noticed a windsock and realised that I was passing Airways flying school at Darley Moor. I turned in immediately and rode up the rough track alongside the grass airstrip. I was delighted to find that Judy Leden was there and on the ground because it was too windy for flying instruction. Judy is an old friend from my hang gliding days, but she had a far more distinguished career in the air than I ever did. More then once she was outright winner of international competitions open to both men and women and was three times Women's World Champion. Now she spends a lot of her time running Airways which probably teaches more people the subtle arts of flight on hang gliders and paragliders than any other school in Britain.

I wetted the plug when trying to get H going again after our cup of tea with Judy. I had become blasé about starting up and the required position for the air on the replacement levers I had fitted was slightly different. A quick plug change and all was well again, but isn't it a bugger how these things always happen when there's an audience...

I was aiming for Coventry and hoping to reach Warwick or Leamington for an overnight stop, but poor navigation conspired against that plan. Ashbourne was no problem, but I eventually found myself in Tamworth at school chucking-out time. The place was choked with cars and children which all seemed to be going in random directions.

The rain started as I was trying to check my map outside the bus depot. By the time I eventually found the back road via Fillongley, it had set in very determinedly, and with it, the belt slip. Plans of getting to the other side of Coventry were increasingly slight as I had to leg it up inclines. I stopped in the forecourt of a village pub which was thoughtfully furnished with huge umbrellas, possibly installed as a direct result of the Met office predicting a 'barbecue summer'. Grounds for legal action there, perhaps. Anyway, they made a perfect shelter while I put the oversuit on. I was about half way through this cumbersome and mildly athletic activity when an amiable local hove into view and opened up with "What is it then?" "A genuine Coventry-built Triumph," I replied, trying to size up whether he was on a mission from the landlord to move me on and hoping that if he was, we may be sufficiently near Coventry for him to be reasonably sympathetic. "Ah, I've always wanted a Bonneville!" he responded. Apparently just the word 'Triumph' had been enough to do the trick, and no, he was nothing to do with the pub, but just passing by. I got the impression that he did a lot of passing by in the village. While I got my suit on and tidied the bike up generally we carried on a wide-ranging and mildly surreal conversation during which, for absolutely no reason I could discern – I had certainly not encouraged the topics in this direction – he remarked “I'm forty-one years old and I didn't have an orgasm until last year.” Fortunately I was just about ready to move on, so I didn't press him for details. H started first kick and I wished him luck with the orgasms and motored away as smartly as we could manage.

The chances of finding somewhere to stay didn't seem too good now, with one promising-looking pub no longer taking guests and the next being fully booked. As I got almost into the middle of the town, through the rain I spotted a sign on a lamp post pointing to 'St Nicholas Street Hotels' and so ended up at the Merrick Lodge. Without that sign I would have been struggling. The hotel was entirely satisfactory and I had a pleasant meal in the bar surrounded by the joyous backwash from an Asian wedding.

Day's mileage: 150 miles
Fuel: Ashbourne 4.38 litres

Holme Moss involves a fair climb to get out of Yorkshire and into Derbyshire

Chapter 16

Who needs a valve lifter?

From the earliest days until the 1960s, motorcycles were often fitted with a manual means of keeping the exhaust valves of the engines open so that they could be turned over relatively easily when getting them started. H is doubly blessed in this department, having a foot-operated half-compression lever and a manual exhaust valve lifter. The first is used exclusively to aid starting and we won't go into the mechanical details here. The second is useful for stopping and assorted operations while in progress. It prevents the exhaust valve from sealing and turns the engine into a rather inefficient air pump which absorbs power rather than producing it.

I find the lever which lifts the exhaust valve is invaluable. It's all down to H's mighty flywheels really. She just doesn't respond to the throttle very sharply at all, so traffic manoeuvres such as braking to enter a roundabout and accelerating to join the traffic flow can easily become a laborious business. The trick is to approach at a comfortable speed, keeping an eye on traffic from the right: if you find you need to shed a few miles an hour, use the valve-lifter, which immediately shuts down the power. As soon as you can, take your place in the traffic flow, drop the valve and the engine starts firing instantly. With a bit of practice you will often find that holding the valve open for just two or three revolutions is all that is necessary. This is much simpler than juggling air and throttle levers, and quicker, too.

The other main use for the valve lifter is when descending long hills. With H being a bit vague in the braking department, the technique is to select a lower gear early on (if it looks really steep, bottom is a good choice) close the throttle completely and lift the exhaust valve while leaving the brake pedal well alone. The engine just pumps away throughout the descent, absorbing energy. The descent is inevitably a slow process which demands patience, but it beats any of the alternatives. One soon learns to scan the countryside well ahead for clues of levelling-out without nasty surprise bends, so that H can be unleashed again at the earliest opportunity.

You may think 'Why bother to close the throttle on descents if simply lifting the valve stops the engine firing?' Well, it doesn't actually stop the engine from firing – it simply stops the charge from being compressed enough to burn properly. In fact, it will try its best to keep firing, with at least partial success because the magneto keeps delivering its spark. Thus, with throttle open and valve lifted, at best your descent will be punctuated with a random succession of spits and bangs. At worst, unburned fuel will congregate in the silencer body until critical mass is achieved and it ignites with great enthusiasm. The result is a backfire which will certainly cause dismay among pedestrians and horses, and may also blow the end off the silencer. I imagine the designers at Triumph discovered this effect early on, because Model H silencers have some concealed slots in them which look suspiciously as if they are there just to relieve such pressure.

So, the valve lifter is the H rider's friend.

Chapter 17

The fliers

Saturday 10 October

Under a grey sky I left Coventry fairly early and in approximately the expected direction. I was glad it was a quiet Saturday as at first, the roads were considerably more major than I like. Eventually, we found Warwick and the quiet road south through the Cotswolds via the Fosse Way. Soon the sky cleared and it was great to be *Hunting the Wren* all the way down the Roman road taking us in exactly the right direction. Moreton-in-Marsh and Stow-on-the-Wold were busy with Saturday shoppers and tourists and we got plenty of smiles and a few waves as H made her way through. Cirencester soon passed and the day turned more and more into something that had been orchestrated by the English Tourist Board. We passed close by the Cotswold airport at Kemble, where F1 cars had been testing only a few days earlier. Airport security has increased insidiously in the last couple of decades and it struck me as quite rare to be able to ride along getting a good view of the runway and parked planes. I liked it.

Another few miles and beneath the sun shining on the White Horse carved into the hillside at Westbury, I spotted some paragliders soaring a couple of hundred feet above the ridge. I kept them in sight for as long as the road would let me, then left them to their airborne pleasure and carried on through picturesque villages on my way to Land's End.

Only a year earlier, I would have wanted to rush up the hill and get airborne too. I know about paragliding. I know that with simple equipment which can be packed in a rucksack it is possible to take a few steps forward into the wind and move effortlessly into the third dimension. I know how to find thermal lift and use it to climb to cloudbase. I have seen Britain from thousands of feet, while supported by no more than a nylon canopy: my local Yorkshire Dales, the Peak District, the Malverns, the South Downs. I have stepped off mountains in Europe, Australia and America. I have made friends with fliers all over the world, but almost exactly a year ago on an October day such as this, as clear as an unopened bottle of Absolut vodka, it all stopped due to the heart attack I related in the introduction.

We pressed on over the Mendips and right through Somerset. H was in great form, coping brilliantly with the hills. Throughout my ride I had not suffered any discourtesy from other road users and I don't believe I had done anything to upset any, either. This changed on a roundabout near Glastonbury where an archetypal white van man carved me up unmercifully, horn blowing, because I was not going quite as fast around it as he could. I do hope he felt better after that.

After a couple of tries, I found a room at the Poacher's Pocket Hotel, close to the Devon border. It couldn't have been better! It had been a perfect day's run. The proprietor's son, Ian Yeo, a keen rider, insisted on moving a bike out of the garage to allow H in. I found that I was in a bit of a hotbed of motorcyclists, which is always reassuring. So was the food. At the end of a long day the home-made minestrone and then venison pie went down very well and I think the lager and a glass of the house red didn't do much harm either.

I felt I was deep into the West Country now and once in bed, set about planning next day's run as usual. I admit it came as a bit of a surprise to see how far away Land's End still was. I had thought that getting there next day would be more-or-less a formality, but now I saw that there was rather more to it than that. Also, I noted that there was no signal on my mobile phone, so I didn't get Trev's usual helpful weather forecast. Never mind, I had a TV in the room and, this being England, the remote control functioned perfectly. None of the forecasts looked very appetising, but then, you never believe what you see on the TV, do you? I was still optimistic.

Day's mileage: 170
Fuel: Warwick 4.2 l litres, Malmesbury 3.1 litres

H had the company of a Triumph Rocket III at the Poacher's Pocket Hotel

Chapter 18

Road kill

One of the pleasures of riding a slow machine down the byways is that you see a lot more wildlife than you do when charging along the motorways.

I was surprised at how widespread the red kite has become. I love to see them soaring, often in pairs. There is something about the way they turn in the air that tells me that it's a kite long before I get a look at those characteristic pointed tails.

On a rainy part of the run up the coast road north of Inverness – I wish I had kept a note of exactly where – we had rounded a corner to see a very large hawk sitting on a post at the corner of a field, only about ten feet from the road. When I say 'large', I mean *really* big! Our eyes were about level. I don't know what sort of an eagle it was, but got a close enough look at its hooked beak to know that it was one of nature's more serious creatures. Could I have seen a golden eagle?

At H's speed most birds and animals can get out of the way without any difficulty, although more than once kamikaze pheasants made a jolly good effort at colliding. We also met a rabbit with a death wish who ran alongside for a long way. As we slowed, so did it, until eventually it darted under our front wheel and into the furthest verge. I don't give much for its long-term prospects.

Sheep were a bit challenging too. Unfortunately, they have been selectively bred for their wool, meat or resistance to the elements. Perhaps it is time that a little effort be directed to producing a variety with at least a vestige of brain or road sense.

It was sobering to see how much of our wildlife does fall to our wheels. Keeping to the nearside at less than 40mph, one gets a close-up of it all. I guess the young deer draped across a verge in the Peak District could top the list. It appeared unmarked and achieved a gracefulness that few animals exhibit in life, let alone as corpses. I counted three badgers, one quite fresh, the others bloated and defiled by road filth. I am not conscious of having seen a badger, alive or dead, up close before. How hairy they are! All those potential top-quality shaving brushes going to waste...

And hedgehogs, but so few. Surely there would have been more twenty years ago? Have our wheels made hedgehogs rare? I do hope not, for a more inoffensive creature is hard to imagine.

The hedgehogs were grossly outnumbered by rabbits and crows. Well, I guess they are crows, but I will hedge my bets by saying 'corvids' generally. Lots of them turn into roadkill, but perhaps that's the price they pay for being carrion eaters who so frequently dine off the tarmac. Here is concentrated symmetry: eat, die eating, get eaten.

Far too many small birds were dead by the roadside, along with occasional pigeon, quail and partridge. I even saw one handsome male black grouse and a soft-feathered owl. Many small mammals of the weasel type had met untimely ends, along with some rats, whose demise leaves me unmoved. Of course, there were some cats too. No doubt they had accounted for a good many birds in their lifetimes, but I still hate to see them run over.

As for insects, well, my ride was late in the season and very few collided with my visor or glasses. It could have been different if I had been travelling a month or so earlier, at the height of the Scottish midge season. I remember what a pest they were on my previous motorcycle venture into Scotland, back in 1973.

Red Kite

© David Cookson Images – with kind permission of David Cookson
www.dc-images.co.uk

Man echoes Nature

No wonder I so admired the red kite!

(A reminder of my hang-gliding days)

Chapter 19

Lanes and rain

Sunday 11 October

There was a farewell committee waiting for me in the Poacher's Pocket car park when I went to get H out of her cosy garage. As well as Ian Yeo, the landlord's son, there was brother-in-law John Bowerman and his daughter Ellie. John had brought another Triumph to see us off. Now, apart from the fact that it would not be inaccurate to describe both H and John's Rocket III as 'Triumph motorcycles', any other similarity is hard to find. H is simple and spare; the Rocket III of the twenty-first century is a masterpiece of excess. It is the Dubai skyscraper of motorcycles. It has three cylinders, each half as big again as H's single one. It has six gears, even though the power and torque are such that just a couple would suffice. It has chromium plating everywhere – something that would not appear for another ten years after H was made: all her bright parts are nickel. It has a total absence of oil leaks. It has liquid cooling and a giant radiator at the front. John's Rocket III could waft me to Land's End in style and luxury, my fingers warmed by its heated grips, the route guided by a SatNav glowing comfortingly on the handlebars, the shaft drive never slipping, no matter how much power I directed to the truck-sized tyre. Would I swap? Nah. I would be overawed by the Rocket's magnificence, whereas H and I have imperceptibly developed what feels like a genuine partnership over the previous thousand-or-so miles. I would miss the affectionate way her air-cooled cylinder radiates warmth to my right calf when things are starting to get a bit much for her, and leave it at that.

With photos, waves and encouragement that there will be dual carriageway almost all the way to Exeter, we were off. Actually, we don't much care for dual carriageways, but it would have felt churlish to say so. It had been a great overnight stop. I wave goodbye to Ian, John and Ellie and get going west, towards a bank of cloud.

I guess that this is as good a point as any to confess that this day was punctuated by a string of route decisions, all of them to a greater or lesser extent, disastrous. Exeter itself was not exactly a joy, the west side of town having been taken over by a sprawl of superstores and modern glass car-dealerships. The main way through seemed to involve an uncanny number of right-angled turns and lavish applications of temporary roadwork traffic lights. When planning the previous evening, I was attracted by the look of a minor road over Dartmoor which would take me through Moretonhampstead and on past Princeton and the brooding gaol. According to Collins' Road Map of Britain, finding the B3212 to Moretonhampstead should have been a formality, but in spite of my best endeavours I ended up on the A30, aiming at Okehampton. That, I thought, would do just as well and the traffic wasn't heavy, so the A30 it was. By Cullompton services a gentle drizzle had started and I stopped to put the oversuit on and enjoy a cup of coffee before deciding to carry on and see what happened. The only way I could have made the day worse would have been if

I had postponed the oversuiting, because the drizzle intensified and soon I was driving into serious rain and spray. The ground rose up and the cloud came down and I was glad that my little bicycle rear-lamp was flashing away on my belt, although I still felt as vulnerable as hell.

Of course, it was only a matter of time before the drive-belt started slipping, which it did, right on cue as I tried to coax H up one of the long exposed climbs. I took the next road off the A30 (they're not called 'slip roads' for nothing) and sheltered under the bridge while I removed a link. My excuse is that an hour or so of the A30 had numbed my brain more than usual and also my hands were cold and wet, but the outcome was that I damaged the rim when re-fitting the belt. OK, you can see where it had been bent and straightened once before during a trial in 2004 and usually I am careful to avoid that area whenever I flip the belt over the flange. This time I wasn't. Bugger. The rim now had a very obvious bend in it, but it went round OK-ish, so I pressed on. The rain persisted and having left the A30 I wasn't keen to go back to it. Surely I would do better to follow the southern coast road, wouldn't I? In the relative comfort of the underpass I consulted the now-soggy remnants of Collins' map and saw that I was on a tiny road which would wend past a village enigmatically named 'Congdon's Shop' and thence to Liskeard, which, again according to Collins, lies at about the same latitude as Torquay. Somehow this excited in me images of palm trees and art-deco architecture drenched in sun, such is the subliminal power of long-forgotten advertising. It all seemed infinitely preferable to sodden Dartmoor, so I set off south. The belt drove fairly well, but a rhythmic clonk from the brake-block, which you may remember shares the same rim as the belt, reminded me that the rim would need further attention sooner rather than later. The rain intensified.

Living close to the Yorkshire Dales I am familiar with hills, but these Devon and Cornish ones are different. Many Yorkshire hills deliver you to a plateau so that the effort of the climb is rewarded by some gentle flattish riding for a while. In the South-West, no sooner have you breasted a summit than you are fighting to keep some sense of order during a precipitous descent. H and I struggled up them one after another and seemed to make little progress Land's End-ward. Although there was still plenty of daylight left, I started to size up the overnight accommodation market, but it was apparent that the task could turn out to be more difficult than I had imagined. Many appealing looking establishments had rain dripping off 'No Vacancies' signs. A month or so earlier that would have meant that they were full of hearty walkers, or at least couples from Bristol conducting shifty affairs, but those signs in mid-October are shorthand for 'the proprietors are off enjoying the profits in Barbados – see you next year'.

I saw a few signs to 'Farmhouse B&B', but as all the farmhouses seemed to lie at the bottoms of steep muddy lanes and I didn't think H had much of a chance of getting back to the road if there were no rooms available, I automatically crossed them off my mental list.

At last we entered Lostwithiel and the overnight decision was made for me. We attacked the hill out of town and lost. As it happened, H ran out of drive virtually on the doorstep of the Best Western Hotel and there we stopped. H was sheeted up in the car park and I took stock of my belongings. They were all wet.

The staff were very welcoming. I thought things were looking up. At reception I fished my wallet out of the inside pocket of my jacket, but as usual the rain had been more then a match for the Belstaff and it was soaking wet. I didn't feel as if I was presenting a particularly dashing figure. A further disappointment was that my credit card was absent. 'Never mind, I have another'. True, but that didn't work because it was six months out of date. 'I can pay cash.' Just as I was about to part with a wedge of Bank of England papier mache I remembered that I also had a debit card and a degree of equilibrium was restored. The receptionist was pretty sharp and volunteered that there was a laundry room with drying facilities. I imagine that my gear pretty well monopolised those facilities that night. And there was still the problem of the missing card. I remembered getting it out to settle up at the Poacher's Pocket that morning (felt like half a lifetime away now) and I could remember John appearing with the Triumph Rocket III at around that time. What I couldn't remember was picking the card up again. Double bugger!

In my comfortable room I experimented with the Corby trouser press as a medium for drying and separating my small moist clump of banknotes. There are better ways. My course record with Corby presses is not good, even when trying to use them for the design purpose. I have invariably managed to add unwanted parallel creases to my trousers rather than emphasise existing ones.

My mobile phone was busy. Word of my travels was beginning to circulate among friends and family. My separated wife, Rosita, whom I am delighted to say is still on good terms with me – was wonderfully supportive. I could have understood if she thought I was crazy, especially as she had played a big part in getting me back on my feet after my heart attack. Apparently there is a bit of amazement among the relatives and she is keeping them up to date. I managed to phone the Poacher's Pocket, and yes, my card was there. Great! I could relax and arranged to call in on my return journey.

This had been a hard day and I feel I sort of 'paid my dues' by pressing on, even though I had probably done fewer than a hundred miles. The forecast for tomorrow is good and I am confident that I will be at Land's End in plenty of time for lunch. It is no further than I have ridden from my home to the start of some vintage rallies. It does turn out to be rather more hilly, though ...

Day's mileage: 95 Miles

Fuel: Exeter 4.67 Litres

Chapter 20

Route finding

The attentive reader will have noticed that the navigational skills I have demonstrated on my meanderings have not been entirely flawless. Apart from the obvious component of basic incompetence, there are many other factors which have made the track-log of my journey look like that of a small yacht in shifting winds. These are:

- My map. In the course of two weeks I managed to destroy two copies of Collins' Road Map of Britain, one through repeatedly trying to read it in the open in pouring rain and the other by cutting it up and fitting strips of it in a route-holder clipped to the handlebars. For overall plotting of the route this map, at 8.7 miles to the inch (5.5km/cm), is excellent. However, for finding your way out of a conurbation, it is hopeless – you need a considerably larger scale, say 4 miles to the inch, to have much chance of success. I persevered with the Collins out of laziness and stupidity, but really I should have got around to buying some more suitable maps.
- Carelessness in my initial map purchase. I set off confidently with the belief that it showed 'Contours in colour', as was written in bold type on the cover. Handy, I thought. It was not until sometime later that I realised that although Yorkshire showed as solid purple it was not in reality a plateau surrounded by precipices. I looked more closely at the cover. It clearly read '*Counties* in colour'... not a lot of help if you are trying to select an easy course through mountains.

- Inability to match speed with other traffic. On wide roads with multiple defined lanes, H's leisurely attitude to accelerating could be a problem. If we found ourselves in the wrong lane among a press of trucks, self-preservation instincts would sometimes stop us from attempting a rapid correction and we would be committed to a less-than-optimal route. However, one way or another we usually got more-or-less where we originally intended.
- Poor signposting. I was trying to travel on the 'old' roads whenever possible – roads that still connect towns and villages but are seen as redundant by travellers trying to get from A to B by motorway. Understandably, the nation's main signposting effort is directed at satisfying the needs of the motorway travellers and little thought is now spent on alternative routes.
- Stupid signposting. Surely the foremost duty of any signpost is to direct travellers in the direction they wish to go as succinctly and clearly as possible. Yet in the north of Scotland that ethos has been abandoned in the name of nationalism. Just try reading the signs on the roundabouts either side of Inverness and you will soon see what I mean. The place names are rendered in Gaelic as well as English and in the same type-size. The Gaelic is in a different colour, but through rain and glasses in the twilight, that is not a lot of help. The overall result was that trying to get onto the right exit felt like trying to decipher the Rosetta stone while banked over, dodging lorries. I'm all for the preservation of Gaelic, which I believe is understood with fluency by about

60,000 folk, the majority of whom live out on islands. No doubt Gaelic has great historic and poetic resonance. I just think that signposts on busy roads are stupid places to be making linguistic political statements.

- The road numbers on the map didn't by any means coincide with reality on the ground all the time. Often there was an extra digit at the end of the 'A' road labels, which tended to throw me, and some of the 'B' roads were completely different. Perhaps I should not grumble about this matter of road numbers; in H's early days there were none in Britain. There was discussion about it before the 1914-18 war, but the system didn't really get under way properly until the early 1920s.
- I didn't have a SatNav or GPS. There were two reasons for this:

a) there is no source of electricity on H apart from the magneto,

b) it would have been totally at variance with the spirit of my endeavour. These are also good reasons why I didn't bother with MP3 players and similar distractions. I did feel a bit of a cheat for taking my mobile phone, but salved my conscience to some extent by rationalising that I would probably be travelling through a lot of country where there was no signal anyway.

- I didn't have a map carrier. I should have rigged up a board on the handlebars where I could display a section of a large-scale map under a sheet of clear plastic. That, coupled with my roller route holder would probably have sharpened up my navigation no end. But, hey, this was supposed to be a bit of an ad-hoc, minimally prepared journey anyway. I got up to the top and down to the bottom and saw a host of interesting things along the way, so it didn't really matter if I didn't hit my route-marks exactly as expected.

Wet, wet, wet in Devon

Chapter 21

To the toe and back

Monday 12 October

My garments retrieved from the drying room, and invigorated by a super breakfast of fresh fruit and kippers (not simultaneously) at the Best Western, I unsheeted H and prepared her for the final miles to Land's End. Morning sun was just nicely driving away the mist. Behind the hotel I found a handy pile of timber off-cuts and decided to try and straighten the badly bent rear belt rim. I slipped the belt off and then found a piece of wood which fitted into the rim quite well, another to wedge it and a heavier chunk to hit it with. Perfect! I hit the rim fairly hard, with no discernible effect. I had another go and thought I saw some improvement. I removed the wedging pieces and spun the wheel: yes! The rim was quite a bit more true. Encouraged that I was on the right lines I jammed the blocks back and set everything up for one last go. After a decent smack I saw to my horror that although the rim appeared even straighter, it now had a nasty radial crack right through the flange. Hmm. The sensible thing would have been to go back down into Lostwithiel and find someone with a TIG or MIG welder who could attempt a patching-up job for me. However, Land's End was in the other direction and I was becoming a bit fixated … I tried a circuit of the car park and the belt drove perfectly well. The crack did not open up. In the end my choice was to press on and try and get it fixed a bit further along my route.

On dry surfaces we climbed the hill out of town. It went on and on, and I was so glad we had given up when we did the evening before. I stopped at St Blazey for fuel and had a good look at the rim. The crack had not developed further and the belt didn't appear to be suffering any more than usual. Land's End was really pulling me now, so under bluer and bluer skies we climbed more hills and descended into more valleys until St Austell, Truro, Redruth and Camborne were behind us. I love the countryside here; love spotting the derelict engine houses of the tin mines and trying to imagine what it must have been like a couple of hundred years ago when Trevithick's great steam beam engines were pumping away. OK, I know that they continued until much, much more recently than that, but it is Richard Trevithick, in every way a larger-than-life character, who is one of my heroes. No railways when he was at work – his engines pumped water from the mines – and the roads were pretty grim too. Yet it can be argued pretty conclusively that he built the first British road locomotive and the first steam railway engine too, although he failed to make a commercial success of either.

It is now October and the tourist season is well and truly over. In Trevithick's day, and until the mid-Victorian period, the ports here in Cornwall would have been busy all the time, coal coming in, tin going out, fish in abundance and all this commerce wind-or-muscle-powered at sea, horse-drawn on land. The severity and frequency of the hills made coastal sailing the most effective way of moving about. So what has become a holiday paradise was not so long ago an industrial landscape.

Penzance presented no problems and the final seven or eight miles were mercifully flat. H was in excellent form and I was singing *Hunting the Wren* inside my helmet. Land's End, the toe of England, shone in the sun and I tried to take a photo from the saddle as we approached. This is not a process I can recommend as it is fairly clearly illegal, but there was no traffic and I thought it worth a try. The result is fuzzy and disappointing.

We were waved through the car-park booth by the attendant saying 'No charge for you.' I'm not clear if that was because H and I were so clearly pensioners, but we appreciated the gesture anyway. Well, this was it. Now I would be able to claim the End-to-End one way at least, but I've always thought of that as only half of the job and to complete it I would have to get back to Leeds under my own steam. I stood H on her stand and was preparing to take a photo when a coach party arrived and a good-natured question-and-answer session was soon under way.

"Where have you come from?" – 'Well, Leeds' (slight pause for dramatic effect – I can't resist hamming it up) – via John o' Groats.' My audience was suitably impressed, I felt.
"And where will you be going?" – 'Back to Leeds.'
"You'll have gone both ways then?" – 'Yes, that's the plan. Gone well so far and I'm enjoying it all.'
"We're from Kidderminster." I was a bit stuck for an answer to that.

Photos were taken and I left H and wandered through to view the attractions of the peninsula. This being the scrag end of the season, there were few visitors apart from the coach party from Kidderminster, who soon disappeared. I had been warned that Land's End was more like Disneyland than Cornwall, that I wouldn't be able to get near the sea, and that it was all a rip-off. I was steeled for something really gross, but in the final analysis I thought it was rather more Sideshow Bob than Disney. It was clean and well-presented and the prices were fair. I bought a fistful of postcards and a large Cornish pasty which I ate while wondering what the connection was between Land's End and Doctor Who, as the enigmatic Doctor and his Tardis figure prominently here. It remains a mystery, but the pasty was excellent.

Soon the promise of a few remaining hours of sunshine set us on the road again. The split in the rim was no worse, so I aimed to go towards Bristol, using the main road for easy miles to start with before diverting to minor routes further on when the main-road traffic thickened up. So it was that we hunted the wren all the way along the A30, over the long drags of Bodmin Moor and up the slopes of Dartmoor. In fine weather and with a fairly major goal having been reached, I allowed my thoughts to range far and wide. The brown tourist-signs to Wadebridge, I noted, offer the rival attractions of Gnome World and the Screech Owl Sanctuary, as well as Port and Starboard Fish and Chips. This is taking specialisation to the outer limits! I visualise long summer queues of little folk in pointy hats patiently waiting for a quarter-scale theme park to open, while down the road screech-owl fanciers with new anoraks and cameras with implausibly long lenses gather for glimpses of their quarry.

Not just any old owls will do for them – it has to be those special screechers! And what about those fish and chip shops? Is 'Port' specifically for left-handed eaters? Is 'Starboard' dedicated to fillets from the right flank of cod or haddock? It is unfair of the tourist authorities to tempt us like this. The public should be told!

Resisting the blandishments of Wadebridge, I soon find myself fantasising about the village of Broadwoodwidger. I cannot be the first to imagine that it must be named after a special tool used by piano tuners. It is so easy to visualise a slim figure in Stevie Wonder glasses pinging a chord on a gleaming concert grand and calling to his faithful dog "Hey, Meg, can you find the Broadwoodwidger in my toolbox – I need to sharpen up this C-major."

With fuel getting low and the light fading, I was relieved to find a 'Services' sign which led me to a Little Chef and a Travelodge. It had been a long day, and I was glad to check in.

Dinner was a satisfactory feed at the Little Chef, and then I settled into my Travelodge room. The bed was huge and comfortable and the TV remote worked flawlessly so I was of a mind to forgive the mould on the bathroom tiles. More intriguing was the electric towel airer which bore a prominent sticker proclaiming *This appliance has been disconnected for your safety*. It had too. When confronted with the problem of (presumably) dangerous electrical installations, it must be a very impoverished management which decides that rather than the obvious remedies of repair, replacement or at the very least, removal, it will take the cheap option of ordering some stickers.

It should have prepared me for tomorrow's breakfast...

Day's mileage: 163
Fuel: St Blazey 4.1 litres, Chiverton 3.67 litres

Land's End at Last!

Chapter 22

Menu mysteries

It has become fashionable to be rather rude about Little Chef restaurants but my experience is that this is a bit unfair. They don't pretend to be anything but basic, and my steak was fine and the apple pie which followed was five-star. While I was eating I scanned the menu and noted how our food and drink vocabulary has changed during my lifetime: so many expressions have joined us from the USA, as well as from more familiar gastronomic sources. From this it was but a short step to imagining what motorcycle tourists of, say, 1920, would have made of many of the Little Chef's offerings. I am pretty sure that a *BLT* would have defeated them and they would have struggled to visualise a *griddled mega combo,* particularly if it was served on a *brioche*. Was *coleslaw* familiar? Did *scampi* and *lasagne* figure on a normal '20s menu? Had *tempura* completed its circular tour of the World, morphing from Portuguese to Japanese and on into English? I suspect not.

I believe the drinks menu would have been equally problematic. Would they have known that a *Coke float* was not a commercial sidecar for smokeless-fuel tradesmen? Would the mysteries of the *cafetière* elude them? What restaurant could have come up with a *cappuccino* or a *latte?* I know that wines have changed too; I don't remember meeting *Pinot Grigio* grapes even twenty years ago and I'm not so sure about *Sauvignon Blanc* either. When did *California Rosé* wine cross the Atlantic?

Seeing the words *Pilsner* and *Carlsberg* on the menu reminded me of something else: all the local breweries that have disappeared since H was built. For our tourist of the twenties, every inn would have been a real-ale pub, probably with just a barrel or two chocked-up against the back wall. The railways would have made a few brewers into national names – Guinness, Bass and Worthington spring to mind – but we would have to wait a generation for the multi-nationals to bring us so much apparent choice and so little real variety.

Chapter 23

Across the Avon

Tuesday 13 October

I slept better at the Travelodge than I can ever remember – ten hours almost straight through. Don't know when I last did that.

When I had checked in, Reception asked if I would like a breakfast delivered to my door in the morning. I knew it wouldn't exactly be a steaming plate of fresh eggs and bacon served on white linen under a silver dome, but even so it sounded like a civilised option and I went for it. As promised, it awaited outside the door and a grimmer feed it would be hard to imagine. Apart from an acceptable bottle of orange juice, there was a capsule of cereal and a little dolly's plastic spoon to eat it with; a chewy strawberry flavoured muesli bar, granular coffee and not much else as far as I can remember. Never mind, you live and learn at this End-to-End game!

Before setting off I changed three of the belt links where the studs were starting to burrow into the fabric. With H fuelled at the Shell Station and topped-up with some 20-50 oil, we were on our way on another clear dry day. I was still vague about the route, but planned to avoid Exeter like the plague and sneak up on Bristol via the A38, remaining on it to Gloucester, where I would strike off for Cheltenham and all points north. My first waypoint was Crediton via the backroads, then to the Poacher's Pocket to pick up my credit card before joining the A38 beyond Tiverton.

On a minor road near Copplestone, I stopped behind a bus. The driver leapt out and for a moment I imagined that my road manners had somehow offended him. Not at all! He was an enthusiast too, and with a load of unfazed passengers waiting, asked about my journey and the bike, rounding off with a couple of photographs. He parted with "That's where I like to see them – not in museums!" My sentiments exactly. The wonderful spontaneity of this encounter made my day.

Arriving at the Poacher's car park at lunchtime I was greeted by a very elderly customer who loudly announced to his companions "Look at that! A Sunbeam. Lovely." Admittedly, the *Triumph* transfers on the tank are very small, but I don't think anyone correctly identified the machine anywhere I stopped. My assurance that H is indeed a Coventry-built Triumph was usually greeted with surprise.

The day was perfect autumn, occasional puffs of wind bringing leaves off the trees; cool, but never cold. With the engine running smoothly we kept *Hunting the Wren* from time to time. The Mendips came and went without drama and in spite of my map-reading shortcomings, we made good progress until Sidcot Hill, just south of Bristol. Traffic had got pretty thick and I rushed the change down to bottom gear, making a really clumsy job of it. The revs soared. Oh, well OK, perhaps 'soared' is overstating H's capabilities, but they did go high enough for the inlet valve to float and close the points of the sparking plug so that she coughed and spat to a standstill. We flopped into a convenient lay-by where I changed the plug and took the opportunity to inspect the crack in the belt-rim. I feared it may have opened up during the climbs of the day, but it looked just as before, so I risked taking a link out – I had been running the belt slightly slack to keep the load as low as possible. Restarting on Sidcot from a dead stop halfway up is a fair test, but all went well and we soon skirted Bristol Airport on our way to the city.

On my map the A38 enters Bristol clearly from the south and emerges equally clearly on the north. I was confident there would be little difficulty in following it through the middle. How wrong I was! I thought I had some idea of my way through as I had visited several times long ago to take photographs for a guide-book to the church of St Mary Redcliffe. And anyway, it was my birthright because my mother had been born in Bristol. My confidence was sorely misplaced.

We swirled around on a grand tour of long-lost Bristol suburbs while the rush-hour built up around us. H coped well, considering, and even an attempt at homicidal assault by Taxi 9090 came to nothing. Somewhat hot and just a bit bothered, we eventually managed to cross the Ring Road to the north and found a comfortable berth at the Swan Hotel. I got a freshly decorated room and H shacked up in a secure garage with a 1300 Yamaha, courtesy of the landlady's partner. Definitely a biker-friendly hotel. I slept wonderfully, but don't know what H may have got up to.

Day's mileage: 128
Fuel: Okehampton 3.26 litres, South Bristol 3.09 litre

If only I hadn't soldered this priming cock closed, I might not have had so much trouble starting at Pathhead (See Page 27)

Chapter 24

The wine-gum calculator

As mentioned in Chapter 3, H needs to be fed engine oil at regular intervals, and this is a matter for the rider as the process is not automated in any way. Contemporary handbooks suggested one stroke of the pump every ten miles, but I prefer a more regular supply of a half-stroke every five miles. That sounds simple enough and in give-and-take motoring five miles takes about ten minutes, so I aim for a shove of the pump at ten-minute intervals. The trouble is that when there is a lot of traffic around and perhaps some navigation to do, it is surprisingly easy to lose one's place. That's when the wine-gum calculator can be helpful.

After years of intensive self-observation I have noticed that on long journeys, assuming I have ready access to an unregulated supply, I am inclined to consume Maynard's Wine Gums at the rate of six per hour. Apparently effortlessly, I can maintain that rate in car, van or motorcycle – if I were religious I guess I would count it as a God-given talent. Anyway, it only took a small leap of imagination to work out that if I were to clip an open bag of Maynards to H's handlebars and encourage my hand to give a half-stroke of the pump every time it was on its way to fish a fresh gum out, both H's appetite and mine would be appropriately satisfied. The system is not entirely flawless and becomes totally useless in rain because wine gums floating in a pool of water lose their magic, but it does help.

By the time I had got back from Land's End I reckon I had got through more than 300 gums. I wonder if this will have been enough to develop a Pavlovian reaction. It will be interesting to see if I'm now programmed to try and press an invisible oil-pump each time I reach for a wine gum during long journeys in my Volkswagen.

It occurs to me that the wine gum is a triumph of misleading advertising: no wine is involved at any stage and as far as the 'gum' part of the name is concerned, the adhesive qualities are sadly lacking. Admittedly a partially chewed one will stick to a woolly sweater for some time, but that is about the extent of it. Transferring them to the mouth from a gloved hand while riding a motorcycle adds an extra layer of mystery to the consumption process, because there is more than a fair chance that you won't have noticed the exact model of gum you have selected. That gives the opportunity to guide your tongue around the lettering on their tops. Even the most uneducated tongue should be able to distinguish 'port' from 'sherry', but some extravagantly named examples are more challenging: the lettering of the longer names is so crammed-in that only a master can decipher them by tongue alone. The implausible 'champagne' struggles to be distinguishable from 'burgundy' against the background of rival distractions caused by traffic pressures and engine-management duties.

Chapter 25

Middle of England

Wednesday 14 October

I reckoned that with a little bit of luck we may just get back to Leeds by tonight. The weather could not have been better and we rode away from the Swan towards the centre of England. This was country I had occasionally visited but didn't really know and I looked forward to what the day would bring.

H was soon into the *Hunting the Wren* rhythm on the easy run up to Gloucester. On long straightish roads such as this, I find that I tend gradually to increase speed because I can see so far ahead and it is clear there are no obstacles. The temptation is to treat the covering of miles as a bit of a formality and let the revs increase to 'get this stretch over-and-done-with as soon as possible'. I try to resist that temptation because it is such a small step to finding oneself hammering the motor on every straight, with all the resultant increases in heat, wear and fuel consumption. Sounds boring, but the slow-and-steady method really does give the best results on a trip such as mine. Gives great time for thought, too.

In Gloucester I encountered my usual route-finding problem. Traffic was light and I did eventually manage to reach Cheltenham without straying onto the M5, but it took a bit of doing. Cheltenham is a beautiful Georgian town and I believe I had the opportunity to admire most of it from several directions before eventually departing on a very minor road to Broadway, rather than going up to Evesham as originally intended. I knew that this alteration would require the ascent of Cleeve Hill, but H was running so well on this beautiful day that I relished the challenge. Sure enough, the old dear did get a bit over-warm about two-thirds of the way up and I thought it best to allow her a rest for a couple of minutes.

It is not unusual for early motorcycles to overheat, especially on long hills, but provided you know the symptoms, no damage need be done. The trick is to recognise loss of power early on and learn to live with it and accept that a really slow climb and/or even a stop and rest may become necessary. The process of coaxing a Model H, or indeed any air-cooled side-valve engined bike of its period, up a hill involves humouring it along in stages. Stage one is to ease the throttle and change smoothly into middle gear. Aim to climb at a steady speed in this gear on no more than two-thirds throttle. Stage two requires you to close the air lever a bit to richen the mixture and retard the ignition a whisker when and if the revs begin to drop off. This Stage two is a bit contradictory, as richening the mixture delivers cooler running, but retarding the ignition makes the engine run hotter but also lets it pull better at low revs; as is so often the case, it is all a matter of judgement and experience. Stage three allows you to give an extra half-stroke of the oil pump regardless of whether your time-and-distance calculations suggest one is necessary. Stage four involves going down into bottom gear which produces a lot of commotion and little else – certainly insufficient forward progress to produce a good flow of cooling air over the engine. If the bike shows signs of really struggling in Stage four, my advice is to stop for a few minutes: it has almost certainly over-heated. The problem is that the iron cylinder is cast in one piece with the cylinder head. The same complicated casting also contains the inlet and exhaust ports and the valve housings, which are all on the same side of the cylinder. Naturally, when that lot really heats up it goes all shapes: soon the cylinder bore becomes somewhat oval and the piston rings can no longer make a good seal. If you stop the engine at this stage and then try the kick-starter, you may be surprised at just how little compression remains. The first time I experienced this I thought I had wrecked the engine – there was so little resistance that it felt as if the piston was missing altogether, but it recovered completely after five minutes or so.

The views from the top of Cleeve Hill were well worth the time and effort invested in climbing it. I love landscapes of all sorts: industrial, maritime, mountain, but these bucolic panoramas of middle-England take some beating. Surely this is indeed England's 'green and pleasant land', as advertised in William Blake's *Jerusalem*. The only problem I have with Blake is just why he and the Women's Institute are so keen to have Jerusalem 'builded here'. I have visited the original and the place is a running sore. A shining example of religious incompatibility and intolerance. My enduring memory is that treading the ancient stones of the Via Dolorosa required the company of a security guard armed with an Uzi sub-machine-gun. The intifada kicked off a month later.

Leave Jerusalem in Israel, I reckon, and don't attempt a replica even if planning permission may be forthcoming…

At Willersey, between Broadway and Stratford on Avon, I found a little gem of a garage right in the middle of the village. It is a time capsule, something to be treasured. I met lots of old-type garages in Scotland, but in England they are increasingly rare. H was given a treat here: a tankful of leaded four-star petrol. She is not really sensitive about the fuel she is given and I don't fuss about it either, rationalising that today's unleaded must be superior to any fuel available when she was designed. However, when some leaded is offered, I tend to buy it as I am persuaded that it may reduce exhaust-valve erosion. Some enthusiasts claim that any contemporary fuels are 'too good' for the low-compression engines of the early vintage years, resulting in incomplete combustion, but I have not found it to be a problem on my old Triumphs.

I pressed on north, towards Coventry and then Derby. Coventry was a nightmare to navigate and my main impression is of wandering into a housing estate with the most vicious speed bumps I have ever encountered. I imagine the Council may have done a deal, which resulted in them being installed free by a local merchant of shock absorbers and steering joints. Nuneaton came next. The art of the signpost has passed Nuneaton by, but I did eventually get on the back road to Derby by dead reckoning alone (the only time this was successful).

After a great run in superb weather, and completely free of belt slip, the way ahead looked ominous. The North was barred by a wall of black cloud, which I interpreted as the start of a warm front, with many miles of rain behind it. The oversuit was indicated, so I stopped at a convenient McDonald's for surprisingly good coffee and a muffin. I gave up on McD's years ago because their coffee was an insult to society, but it has improved greatly since then. I took the opportunity to phone Ian and get a weather report from Bradford. The news was good: no rain, so the front wasn't as bad as it looked. Home still seemed to be just within reach given an easy run and a dry belt.

Traffic was really thick in Derby, which I intended to leave on the A61, for Sheffield, Barnsley, Wakefield and Leeds. I first drove up this road in 1960, at the wheel of a 1938 Ford 8, with new wife inside and ironing board tied to the roof as we travelled from London to set up home in Yorkshire. In those days when the M1 petered out near Rugby, the A61 was the only alternative to the A1.

Although busy, Derby was fun because I teamed up with a jovial pair of Asian taxi drivers who were fascinated by my machine and project. A cab each side of me, we sustained a disjointed and surreal conversation through several sets of traffic lights as they shepherded me onto the exit to the A61. Thank you gentlemen!

The road north was a lot less fun than the taxi drivers, and I soon decided that it was too much of a trunk-road racetrack for H and me. I also had to admit that Leeds before lighting-up time was a bit optimistic and prepared for another stop. Fuel was getting low, too. Soon a sign appeared listing the spa delights of Matlock and I decided to surrender to its temptations. I found a garage eventually, but a bed proved more difficult. The first three hotels I tried were either full, non-residential, considered the season over, or didn't like the look of a tired biker. The fourth seemed to be just what I was looking for but the bed and breakfast rate was pretty high. 'Well, all our rooms are doubles' the receptionist explained and was not prepared to offer a reduced rate for single occupancy. I was buggered if I was going to pay for two breakfasts, so I moved on. I do not claim to be an expert on the economics of tourism, but Matlock Bath on a grey October evening did not appear to be exactly teeming with potential guests, so I'm surprised that she turned me down, losing a restaurant and bar customer too. Maybe she didn't like the look of a tired biker, either.

Fortunately there was a fish restaurant nearby, with rooms on offer, and I settled there most comfortably. Secure parking is hard to find in Matlock Bath, so H was wheeled under the umbrellas at the front of the restaurant, sheeted-up and chained to a drainpipe. She seemed quite happy with that arrangement.

Matlock is about as far from the sea as it is possible to get in England, but my poached cod was perfect: it tasted is if it had been landed that morning. I am a great fan of traditional fish and chips, with the fish cooked in batter, but my 'keep-the-heart-running-a-bit-longer' diet has made me pick the non-fried option more frequently: rarely has it been as good as this!

160 Miles
Willersley 4.6 litres Matlock 3.43 litres

H's overnight drainpipe at Matlock Bath

The centre of commotion

Chapter 26

A little history

As motorcycling developed during the first decade of the Twentieth Century, so did the chasing of records from End-to-End. There was no finer way of demonstrating the speed and durability of these new powered bicycles, although at first they were neither speedy nor durable! This was a marketing opportunity of the first order which is clearly seen when you consider the impact motoring was having on society at that time. Cars were becoming fairly reliable – apart from the perpetual tyre problems – but they were so expensive that only the seriously wealthy could afford to run one, and such people tended to employ chauffeurs anyway. Motorcycles were altogether a different proposition: the cost put them within the reach of great swathes of the middle classes and they could be stored in the smallest shed or outhouse. By 1905-6 the motorcycle's potential market was huge, but then as now, there was a bit of an image problem and sales were hard to come by. The trouble was that the early models really had been chronically unreliable, due in great part to the haphazard nature of their ignition systems which tended to rely on batteries capable of disintegrating after only a few miles of rattling over unsurfaced roads on unsprung bikes. Also, the methods of feeding petrol and air to the engines were rather vague, the so called 'surface' carburettors consisting of little more than a small sub-tank for some fuel, through or over which air was encouraged to pass on the assumption that it would absorb a combustible proportion of flammable vapour on its way. Small surprise then that the bikes were tricky to start, extremely sensitive to throttle settings once under way and prone to catching fire if the battery hadn't already packed up. This introduced a glorious perversity whereby the agitation the fuel received when travelling rough roads tended to induce the engine to run more willingly than when on dead smooth stretches. All this must have become astonishingly wearing, and that any riders at all managed End-to-End runs on such equipment is amazing, but, as the records show, a few did!

From around 1906 technology had progressed to the point where the basic problems were over: the high-tension magneto pioneered by Robert Bosch in Germany was proving ideal for motorcycles and spray carburettors, mainly drawing on experience of the French *Longuemare* type, were in general use. Unfortunately the initial unfavourable image persisted and although the public's enthusiasm for parting with money for impractical machines had waned, not everyone had lost faith. The ACC, forerunner of the Auto Cycle Union, organised a six-day reliability trial from Land's End to John o' Groats in which more than 70 motorcycles, tricars and cyclecars started and two-thirds of them completed the course. According to *The Motor Cycle* magazine this competition was the 'most important ever organised for the encouragement and development of motor cycling. The distance over which it extends, the diversity of the country traversed, the number of entries received, and the actual number of starters amply justify this statement.'

The event received huge support and was widely reported nationally. In a country where the roads generally could not be closed for racing, Land's End to John o' Groats took on a prominence in the minds of the public which would last until 1911. Crack riders were being sponsored by motorcycle manufacturers and receiving contingency payments from accessory suppliers.

The route was usually ridden from north to south and naturally, the record-breaking season was centred around mid-summer, to take advantage of the short nights – daybreak at John o' Groats could be as early as 3.00 am and sometimes the northern sky never became seriously dark. Even so, at the end of the first day the riders would be confronted by the need to ride at full speed over unlit roads for some hours, the way ahead lit only by their acetylene headlights.

By 1909 Ivan Hart-Davies, an amateur rider, but with works support, had the time down to 33hr 22m on a 3.1/2hp Triumph. That time was fast enough to discourage many other hopefuls, and those who did try to beat it failed in one way or another. Then, at the end of the 1910 season, Arthur Moorhouse carved an hour off Ivan's time, covering the distance on a Rex in just 32hr 20m. That was particularly remarkable as he didn't set off until September 20th, when the daylight hours were considered too few by virtually everyone else. Hart-Davies presumably spent the winter plotting to regain his record and by June 1911 he was fully prepared for what was to turn out as the grand finale of motorcycle record breaking on British roads. His mount was once again a 3.1/2 hp Triumph and he was supported by the Triumph company. He completed the route in only 29hr.12m.

Hart-Davies' meticulous approach to getting from end to end contrasts sharply with my own spontaneous and unfocused method. Like the other serious record-chasers he established depots at regular intervals with supplies of fuel, oil, spares and refreshment. His bike had no gearbox, but he could vary the drive reduction ratio by adjusting the flanges of the engine pulley. That was easier said than done, as it involved stopping, removing the belt, using a spanner on the pulley and then fitting another belt to suit the changed ratio. Typically, a low ratio of 6:1 would be used for the hilly sections and 4.5:1 for the flatter parts. He would have been carrying at least two belts and there were extra ones at the supply depots.

At critical junctions men were stationed to point the correct route and for much of the ride he would be led by 'pacers' – local racing motorcyclists who knew their stretch of the road inside-out. The depots were usually positioned at hotels and the whole chain kept in touch by telephone so that his progress could be plotted and arrival anticipated. He needed all this backup, not least because his pace put terrific demands on his tyres. Covers and tubes were consumed in quantity and even so he had to push-in the final mile and a quarter to Land's End on foot because his last tube was terminally punctured. I don't like to imagine what that must have felt like after averaging 30mph over rutted roads on a fundamentally unsprung motorcycle for more than a day and a night.

The bike manufacturers and various suppliers of fuel and equipment took advertising space in the motorcycle magazines of the period to trumpet the achievements of such as Ivan Hart-Davies. After all, that was the main point of the exercise. There was, however, a major snag: the blanket speed limit on British roads was then only 20mph. I don't know exactly when certain authorities began to put two and two together and draw the inevitable conclusion that the limit was being treated with contempt, but in 1911 the Auto Cycle Union announced that it would not recognise any further claims and the heroic period ended. From then on the TT races and Brooklands circuit, both of which got under way in 1907, would be unchallenged as the national showcases for motorcycle performance.

Just to show that I didn't come to any lasting harm on the "End to End" escapade, here I am on Sunday 20th March 2011 taking part in the Pioneer Run from Epsom to Brighton. I'm riding my other *Trusty Triumph,* a 1913 Type C.

Photo courtesy of Nick Jonckheere

Chapter 27

Home

Thursday 15 October

My bedroom above the cafe incorporated a huge double bed and was spacious and comfortable. I had an excellent night. There was, however, one curious feature: a small toilet cubicle which was fitted with a floor-to-ceiling louvre door, not really an auspicious choice. The spacing between the slats was generous to the extent any activity within the cubicle would be equally apparent outside it. Potentially a bit of a passion-killer, that.

Full of egg and bacon, I motored H away down Matlock Bath's main street through a vague morning drizzle.

My route home soon took me via the sumptuous grounds of the Chatsworth estate, a process that brings to the surface the latent Marxist within me. I vault my imagination forward a couple of centuries and wonder if the proles will be invited to view 1990s Russian oligarchs' yachts with similar reverence. I am simply not a stately homes-type person. OK, I acknowledge that their construction provided employment for many and that craftsmen and artists found work that may not have been available elsewhere, but I find the extravagance loathsome. Would I tear them down? No, but why the National Trust has to preserve *quite* so many is beyond me.

Then it was out to Hathersage and along beside the Derwent valley reservoirs where the Dambusters honed their bombing skills flying Lancasters built a mile or so from my Leeds home. I reflected how grateful we should be to Tony Blair for keeping our militaristic traditions so vividly alive with his initiatives in Iraq and Afghanistan. Maybe.

In spite of dampness, H's belt kept driving well up the big hill towards Sheffield. I intended to miss the city by taking the Strines road to Bradfield and Stocksbridge. However, when the turning came up I found myself in cloud with very poor visibility and selected the less-chancy option of going straight on down the Rivlin valley to Sheffield where it was drizzling nicely. Sheffield is one of the few English towns with a modern tramway system, so I was able to get full value from the narrow-tyres-on-wet-tramlines experience which was so common in H's youth. Then we soon picked up the A61 again and motored in style past Sheffield Wednesday's stadium and on over the hills to Barnsley on drying surfaces.

Here the road was fairly quiet, all the commercial traffic having been bled off onto the parallel M1, and I enjoyed the ride. Barnsley was generously and accurately signposted. Nuneaton's councillors on their roads committee should send a study group to Barnsley to see how it can be done, but I guess they are too busy trying to study their own bottoms without the benefit of a mirror.

More long hills took me past Newmiller Dam to Wakefield. All the way I was feeling more comfortable. I was firmly back in West Yorkshire and this really felt like home ground. I know the route through Wakefield well enough. I used to have to come here frequently to deal with matters of vehicle registration, but that happens in Leeds now.

On the rather dull road between Wakefield and Leeds the main attraction is a weathered arch constructed from the jawbones of a whale. Just before I set out I had read an excellent book relating the tale of the whaling boat *Essex* in the early nineteenth century. This was reputedly Herman Melville's inspiration for Moby Dick, and a more grim existence I find hard to imagine. Even without the sinking and the cannibalism it would be way beyond the limits of any journey I would care to undertake. The thought of it rather put my current endeavour into perspective!

At the top of the final hill the sun broke through to illuminate the Civic Hall and high-rises of Leeds so that the city put on a transitory appearance as the Promised Land.

I am grateful that I know Leeds well, because its road plan looks like a wiring diagram for Christmas lighting and navigating from one side to the other is probably as mystifying to visitors as I found Bristol and Nuneaton put together. Now I had virtually completed my run and to reach home had to choose between the Ring Road or going right through the middle. 'We'll do it in style' I thought and chose the City Square route. The god of traffic lights smiled upon us all the way as we passed through the lunchtime crowds, past the Black Prince's statue in front of the Queens Hotel and out of town to the west. Just six miles to go!

I rode out alongside the bulk of Kirkstall Abbey, up the hill to Horsforth, over the Ring Road, past the crematorium and the abattoir (it's nice to have landmarks) until, just as I reached the bottom of the final rise to my house, H ran out of power.

I had to pull on to the pavement and humour her to finish the remaining hundred yards of the End-to-End under her own steam. While I was checking the plug, quite by chance another H owner, Robert Davis from nearby Otley, pulled up in his car to offer help. We could have pushed-in easily, but I was determined that H should finish those final steep yards under her own power. The plug was fine, but there was virtually no compression. I think it was my fault: my mind being on other things at the end of my two thousand miles I hadn't given her enough oil on the final steady climb out of Leeds to my suburb and she had simply overheated. After five minutes and a pump of oil, normal service was restored and we motored up to my garage door without any difficulty. H and I had done it!

Day's mileage: 70
As near as I could measure, 1.1 litres of fuel was left in the tank.

Chapter 28

Well, What was that all about?

On the face of it this really was a pretty stupid thing to do. The journey was the object. Simply the matter of going from *A* to *B*, to *C* and back to *A* again. I didn't have to do it faster than anyone else or meet any deadlines. And, apart from for my own satisfaction, I didn't even *have* to complete it, but my mindset made me pretty determined. I would get H up and down the course if I possibly could and would have looked upon calling out any of the get-you-home services as an act verging on humiliation.

I was often asked if I was doing it all for charity and my answer was that I was not. There were many reasons, not least of which was that I did it almost at the drop of a hat. Apart from that, I wasn't comfortable with the concept of asking lots of people to reward me for having a jolly good time! However, I did make a pact with myself that I would make a donation to the British Heart Foundation if I pulled it off. This worked well, because writing out the cheque in the afterglow of success was unusually painless. An unexpected spin-off was that I was asked to join the BHF's list of speakers when news of my jaunt leaked out. I confess that I wasn't exactly shy when it came to the leaking, but I was surprised at the amount of press coverage one local phone call led to. I am pleased to have been asked to speak and H and I will no doubt be inflicting ourselves on Rotary clubs throughout the parish for some time to come!

I was also asked if it was dangerous. That's a harder one to answer, because if one looks at the project dispassionately it has to be admitted that there was a degree of exposure which would have been missing if I had stayed at home seeing the country from the sofa via GoogleEarth. The only problem with the simulator solution is that it misses the whole purpose of experience. I am a passionate believer in real experience and take a stereotypical grumpy old man view of computer games. In my world no amount of time swiping at thin air in your sitting room on a Wii can compare with taking a real corner on a real motorcycle, skiing on real snow, feeling the tug of the harness as a paraglider launches, or even hitting a real tennis ball. And anyway, once you have reached seventy you should be allowed to stick your neck out as far as you like – encouraged to, even! We oldies have so much less to lose and our deaths should be seen as mild surprises rather than as tragedies.

Taking a slow trip on the roads the length of England and Scotland showed me how our society is changing irresistibly, in a way that motorway travel does not reveal. So many boarded-up pubs and so many superstores on estates which make the suburbs of Exeter and Inverness indistinguishable until you get out of the car and listen to the accents.

If there was ever any doubt that the motor vehicle has come to dominate our transport systems, a glance at the average street will give the game away. I have not seen any estimate of the amount of white and yellow line material that has been spread throughout the country, but I bet it would be several Albert-Halls-full, or whatever the standard unit of measurement is. Some of the marking was lumpy and slippery as hell under the tyres when wet. We seem to have reached the stage where people are incapable of gauging where the edge of the road is and driving accordingly. Now, apparently, all the roads have to be as clearly defined as the lanes on athletic tracks. I found it was a delight and a relief to ride along byways so insignificant that the local highways committee had deigned to overlook them. I also applaud the way the semi-obsolete mainish routes such as the old A6 are slowly reverting to nature because their arterial status is long gone, claimed now by their Motorway cousins, and their white-line budgets gone too. The risk is that in a few years time these roads will have become potholed relics, fit only for 4-WDs and trail-bikes, but at present they are just right, so make the most of them.

Parking has changed too: car ownership is so endemic that the old offence of 'obstructing the highway' has all-but disappeared in many small towns, to the extent that even quite important through-routes have become intermittent one-way streets, the direction of flow depending on the goodwill or weak resolve of the participants at any particular moment.

Having no radio gives a great opportunity for reflective thought. I would find myself motoring along gently while compiling mental lists. One of my favourites was a list of images which really irritate me. Samples (in completely random order) include Sir Alec Ferguson, who presumably got his knighthood for services to the chewing-gum industry – the romance of football is lost on me; the parasitic bishops who sit in the House of Lords and influence our laws without any credible mandate at all; and consider royalty – an ethnic minority by any standards, yet inexplicably the subject of wholesale discrimination – *positive* discrimination admittedly – but I thought we are supposed to be striving towards a society in which all forms of discrimination are outlawed! The beauty of occupying occasionally boring stretches of road with this innocent pastime brings all sorts of satisfyingly grotesque images to mind, images which may otherwise have passed by quite forgotten. Such gems as Sir Cliff Richard on that wet day at Wimbledon, or another 'Sir' – Jimmy Savile, doing virtually anything.

It has taken me years to realise that Savile was a pioneer of the current fashion for achieving celebrity without any perceptible talent, but I'm not sure if he deserves respect for that.

And that brings me to one more list that I found depressingly easy to compile: dodgy politicians! Far too long to go into in this book, although I am moved to make an exception for one of 'Blair's Babes' – the allegedly expenses-wangling Hazel Blears. In my eyes, she managed to infect both politics and motorcycling with questionable morality in one brief TV clip when, dressed in an admittedly cute set of leathers, she swept past reporters and escaped their questions on the pillion of a bike.

A particular thing which struck me is the sheer number of war memorials we have. I mentioned the one at Berriedale earlier on. It is a huge monument when seen against the scale of the village, but it needed to be because of the number of names that had travelled from this far-northern region to get killed on behalf of the Union. That image was repeated time after time as H and I made our way up and down the island. From Motorways you don't see many war memorials – probably none at all, but on a slow meander you meet them at village after village, town after town. The memorials really began to get to me: we become so familiar with those in our immediate neighbourhoods that if you are like me you scarcely notice them and rarely think about them. I wish that Tony Blair and George Bush could have visited a few dozen before they prayed together to their god and went on to commit holy war in far countries ostensibly on behalf of me and the rest of their respective electorates.

I wonder what all those closed pubs say about how we live now? Should we see each as a sort of campaign medal for the drink-drive and anti-smoking campaigns, or as a loss to society? Maybe they are shrines to the success of supermarkets' '24 cans of Stella for the price of a fresh lettuce' philosophy.

The trip illustrated starkly just how much a country changes in a lifetime. When I moved up to Yorkshire in 1960, one of the mills I visited still bore evidence of Luddite activity. The textile industry was still going strong and I learned a whole new vocabulary of job descriptions which are again forgotten. Not much chance now of meeting a burler or a mender, let alone a doffer or loom-tuner on your way from Tesco to the multiplex cinema. No longer is the night sky illuminated by steelworks from Sheffield to Rotherham – that task is left to the neon of the Meadowhall retail park these days. I don't mourn these changes but simply note them as changes. Just that. It is change itself which is normal. If by some strange mechanism Britain had not changed in my seventy-odd years, let alone H's ninety-plus, it would be a strange place indeed – a sort of mega museum, a National Trusty theme park.

....

A couple of days after my return I was asked to ride H for a few press photographs. She was untouched since my return – I had been busy catching up with phones and letters again. She kicked into life first go and off we went up the road. 'Can you turn there … can you stop here"... and so on. I could; I didn't even have to think about it. I didn't appreciate how fluent I had become at coaxing H along. I felt completely at home, in my element, like a performer who only really comes to life on the stage. I reckon H and I can travel any road, anywhere …

The final figures

I calculate I covered at least 1,989 miles on my journey. I had no odometer and have taken the mileages from the AA's website route finder. I have made allowances for the erratic nature of my navigation, but I have been fairly conservative in this and I don't think the distances are far out.

I bought just short of 90 litres of petrol, and bearing in mind the litre I had left, I believe that translates to near-enough 19.5 imperial gallons to complete the trip. That yields 102 mpg. I am very impressed by that. Oil consumption was less impressive, due to the total-loss nature of the system. I didn't keep a check on it, but I am sure I used less than a gallon – say four litres at most.

My body suffered little from its ordeal. My repaired heart didn't let me down at all and I simply didn't worry about it. I had a cooked breakfast most days but very light lunches – sometimes only a chocolate bar and a coffee. In the evenings I would have a good dinner and kept a fairly tight rein on the alcohol because I didn't fancy setting off with a hangover. Altogether I lost a couple of pounds – about a kilo. A surprise side effect was that after a couple of weeks sitting to attention on H's saddle, my back, which is prone to miserable sessions of sacroiliac torture, gave me less aggro than I have known for years. After a few days crouched over a word processor it is back to normal. There is a message there, somewhere!

A last surprise

I tackled the run simply for my own satisfaction and consequently was surprised when I discovered that I was to be put forward as a candidate for the Vintage Motor Cycle Club's premier award, *The Karslake Memorial Trophy*, better known as the *Dreadnought Trophy*, presented for the year's best performance on any eligible machine. I hope you can imagine my delight when I received the phone call telling me that I had been successful. The perfect end to a long ride.

The Dreadnought Trophy

Postscript

Hunting the Wren

The folk song which kept coming into my head during the run apparently originated in East Anglia. Or Ireland. Or the Isle of Man. It all depends which website you search on! As with so many of the old songs, the history is a little muddy. Anyway, the version I like is a repetitive sort of 'chant and response' song which fits the beat of an easy running Model H Triumph. It goes rather like this:

"We'll hunt the wren", said Richard to Robin
"We'll hunt the wren", said Robin, a-bobbin'
"We'll hunt the wren", said Jack o' the land
"We'll hunt the wren", says everyone!

"And where shall we find 'im?" said Richard to Robin
"And where shall we find 'im?" said Robin, a-bobbin' … etc

"In yonder green bush", said Richard to Robin …

"And how shall we kill 'im? said Richard to Robin …

"With arrows and bows", said Richard to Robin …

"And how get 'im home?" said Richard to Robin ...

"The brewer's big cart!" said Richard to Robin …

"How will we cook 'im?" said Richard to Robin …

"In a big copper pot, " said Richard to Robin …

"And how'll we eat 'im?" said Richard to Robin …

"With knives and forks," said Richard to Robin …

"Who'll come to the dinner?" said Richard to Robin …

"The King and the Queen," said Richard to Robin …
"The King and the Queen," said Robin, a-bobbin' ..
"The King and the Queen," said Jack o' the land
"The King and the Queen," says everyone!

"Eyes to the blind
Legs to the lame
Alms to the poor
Bones to the dogs," says everyone!

Acknowledgements

This is the story of a one-man expedition which was done without any on-the-road support. In case this gives the impression that I could have completed the journey and produced this narrative without help, I now put the record straight. I thank all the following:

Ian Jennings who keeps my bikes running by using engineering solutions as antidotes to my own inelegant spanner-work. The late Colin Missen for generously lending me historical End-to-End material which he had assembled in connection with his own runs and which I have plagiarised mercilessly. Trevor Birkbeck, for encouragement and feeding me with weather information as well as providing the bed which got me on my way. The Whittall boys, Matthew and Robert, for supporting my writing resolve past the first couple of chapters. Paul Foggitt for access to his father's war diary. Peter Liddle for introducing me to Stan Sharp, my publisher. Rosita Whittall as proof-reader par excellence. Gail Gilliland for constructive criticism of the text and Bob Wylde who a week or so before the run, had trued the rim and re-tensioned the spokes in H's front wheel at a moment's notice to get her through her MOT.

And finally, heartfelt thanks to all my dear friends in the vintage motorcycle movement who nominated me for the Dreadnought Trophy.